How Great a Crime

–to speak the truth

The story of Joseph and Winifred Gales
and the *Sheffield Register*

How Great a Crime – to speak the truth

The story of Joseph and Winifred Gales
and the *Sheffield Register*

www.1889books.co.uk

ISBN: 978-0-9935762-6-3

Neil Kay
1936 - 2015

Foreword

My dad started to write this story in the early 2000s and had a working draft in a reasonable sort of shape when he suffered another serious setback in health. It was always his intention to finish this book, and I used to ask him about it – especially after I'd taken up writing more seriously, and indie-publishing books. He always gave the impression he was close to finishing it, but never did; then he had further ill health. He died in November 2015.

After some time had passed, I sat down to look through the manuscript. Dad had worked almost exclusively off the microfilm copies of the *Sheffield Register* and from printed material. In the last few years, however, additional sources of information have become available, primarily the digitised memoir of Winifred Gales, the "Recollections," made available by the University of North Carolina, in addition to several recent academic works published online. I have used these to review and add to my father's original work.

The project has not been some sort of sentimental journey. My interest has been that of a storyteller, looking at a lost story and wanting to see it told – that is one of the things I do in my writing and publishing: especially when it relates so closely to Sheffield.

Joseph Gales was one of the all-time great Sheffielders –forget Joe Cocker, Jessica Ennis-Hill, Sean Bean or Michael Palin. These are all minnows compared to Joseph Gales – and their stories are boring besides that of the Galeses. Their story has been forgotten and has not been brought together in one place before. This story is not just something dredged up from history – an irrelevant dusty skeleton.

What the Galeses tried to do for freedom of the press, and for free speech – principles for which they had to flee the country, principles which they took with them to America and put into practice there – is something which will resonate today. We have seen the Free Press demonised and accused of "fake news" just for holding up the mirror of truth (not "alternative truth") to power.

The Galeses, founding citizens of the United States, believed in Parliament being held to account by the people – they would have much to say today where the votes of 37% of the electorate in the

UK are held up as being an "overwhelming mandate" to push one of the most momentous, critical decisions taken by government in decades, and which has nothing to do with returning power to people, but further restricting it. (There is more than a hint of the rotten boroughs still hanging over British "democracy.") In many ways we have made progress but in many ways we are taking retrograde steps, and under threat of losing hard-won liberties. Joseph and Winifred Gales are very relevant 230 years on.

A note on the text

This is a story-telling, not an academic thesis. I have therefore omitted footnotes and long debates on sources. I am not a historian by background, but my academic training was scientific and my career is in legal enforcement, so evidence matters to me. Where there is very weak evidence I have left things out, where the evidence is irrefutable or beyond reasonable doubt I have included it, where it is equivocal but interesting, I have tried to make it clear in the text.

The principal sources relied on can be found in the References at the back. You can leave comments or ask questions at www.theevergreen.co.uk/how-great-a-crime.

Some of these sources are more reliable than others – the Montgomery memoir is clearly not objective and aims to justify the youthful actions of the, by 1854, quasi-saintly and establishment figure of James Montgomery: their line being that he was basically a young innocent lead astray (a line which doesn't stand up to examination of the evidence). Writing of his time at the *Register*, Montgomery said he was "ignorant of myself and inexperienced in the world as a child of seven years old." Of his early reformist writing he says: "he had been one of the greatest fools that ever obtruded himself on the public notice." His biographers write: "Tears of repentance, as honourable to the man as they were becoming in the Christian, were afterwards shed for the 'sins of his youth.' " It therefore has to be read with an understanding of this revisionist filter. Above all, the writings of the Galeses themselves, through the newspaper and the "Recollections," is relied upon most

– there is incredible consistency of opinion and temperament throughout, from the early editorials through to the writings of the later years.

The "Recollections" is an incredibly rich source of information, it was written over a number of years by Winifred. After her death, Joseph himself, in his later years, finished the manuscript, wanting to fill in one or two gaps. It was started as a family memoir to pass on to future generations in their family. It was never intended for publication; in fact, Winifred said that it was intended for their offspring and a few candid friends, and for them only. She continued: " I hope and believe that all my children have too just a concept of what is right, for any of them to wish to make any part of this family narrative public but lest any of them at a remoter period, (for I flatter myself that my children's children will find some pleasure in the perusal) should be so misled, I here put an absolute and solemn veto upon such an act of folly in them – and injustice towards me."

That these wishes have been overridden with the passage of time is fortunate – their legacy was so much more than that given to their offspring.

Introduction

At the end of the 18th century Britain was at a crossroads – one way led to parliamentary reform and a forward-looking society based on equality of rights and a representative government, the other way led to repression and fear as the privileged few sought to cling to power. The latter route was the one the country chose, or was pushed down, depending how you look at it, as Pitt's government swung its iron fist. The result set the country back decades and resulted in a huge loss of talent.

Several factors influenced the outcome. Principally, the stranglehold of the aristocracy on the levers of power combined with their unerring belief in their right to rule. Added to this, those men of influence who might once have been prepared to countenance change, shied away from reform when faced with sheer panic at what happened in France's Reign of Terror. Then, there is something in the British, that has always made the idea of violent revolution distasteful to a large part of the population, or perhaps a sense that it's really not worth all the effort and fuss. In the end, everyone of influence who did not support the status quo, and who dared to question parliament or the king were locked up, transported, cowed – or they fled abroad, largely to America.

Joseph Gales and his wife Winifred were amongst the greats of the era who let reason and truth be their guide. The Gales' seven years of publishing and editing *The Sheffield Register* were a remarkable achievement. Their flight to America along with that of many other great people was a huge loss to Britain and it can only be imagined what more they could have achieved, and how much better Britain and Sheffield would have been, had they stayed.

Joseph Gales was a moderate, non-conformist Christian with strong, moral values, and who hated all forms of violence and disorder. He was deeply committed to the freedom of the press and maintaining its role in challenging abuses of power. He was a man who had a deep sense of personal honour, and who felt he must live by his principles and convictions.

Over the period of the newspaper's publication he was drawn more and more into political campaigning in favour of parliamentary reform and defence of liberty. This provoked an intense and sometimes vicious local enmity amongst a small section of the local community with links to representatives and agencies of government, setting a process in motion which almost resulted in tragic consequences for Gales and his family.

Alongside Benjamin Flowers of Cambridge, Gales is credited with being the first editor of a provincial newspaper to incorporate in his columns original news stories, including stories covering local events and issues, along with editorial comment. The newspaper is a fund of fascinating information about Sheffield life and issues in the late eighteenth century, but over its last five years it goes well beyond this. Sheffield was one of the places where the late 18th century clash of ideologies played out the strongest.

Early Years

Joseph Gales was born in Eckington, just outside Sheffield on the 4th of February 1761, the first child of Thomas Gales and Sarah Smart. Thomas Gales started out as a last-maker, but before long took up the trade of running a public house and brewing beer which brought in sufficient money to educate Joseph, his brother, and three sisters. When he was 13 years old he was apprenticed to a book and stationery store in Manchester run by a Mr and Mrs Prescott. He was bound as an apprentice for 7 years – apprentices were legally tied to their masters back then. He was treated badly and sought help from his uncle who lived in the town. Prescott was taken to court, but young Gales was not released from his indentures; instead Prescott was only reprimanded and told if there was any future complaint the indentures would be annulled. On his return Joseph was again whipped and badly treated, and, after several more months, again got his employer summoned to court – he also complained that he was not getting the instruction in the business he was supposed to be getting. The magistrate ordered the indentures to be cancelled, but Prescott appealed to the county court – delaying the decision a further three months.

Young Gales could not wait that long, so he set off walking the 50 miles back home to Eckington.

It was then that a neighbour of the Gales family put them in touch with a printer and bookseller in Newark by the name of Tomlinson, who took Joseph on for the remainder of his apprenticeship. He won the county court case in Manchester and was freed to pursue his career in Newark.

Tomlinson was, in addition to being a printer and bookseller, a dealer in carpets and wallpaper. He was also an auctioneer and appraiser (roles that often went hand in hand with printing in those days). And he ran a circulating library – it was through this that Gales met Winifred Marshall, a keen reader. Winifred was the daughter of John and Elizabeth Marshall, and was, just a few months younger than Joseph. His work also enabled Gales to continue his own self-education: both reading and discussing books with educated customers.

One work that had an important influence on Gales was a pamphlet that Tomlinson printed in 1782 or 1783 by the Rev. Dr Disney, giving his reasons for resigning his church living over his lack of support for the doctrine of the Trinity. Gales subsequent association with the Unitarian church was pivotal to his outlook on life.

Two years after his apprenticeship finished, Gales went about setting up his own printing business in Sheffield with a view to marrying Winifred. He did this on money he had saved, together with a small amount of Winifred's inheritance from her father's estate. (Winifred was born into a well-to-do family, her grandmother's cousin being Lord Melbourne.) More importantly than the money, in his own words, was a character of being "an industrial, upright businessman." He had developed contacts in London and got ready loans to set himself up.

Joseph and Winifred married on the 4th of May 1784 – they lived above their shop in Hartshead, which was then a busy thoroughfare in the town. Arthur Jewitt, a contemporary, described their premises as being "at the top of the narrow street leading from the top of the Hartshead to Friends Meeting House." Winifred ran the shop, selling books, stationery and patent medicines, whilst Joseph ran the office, printing and auctioneering businesses. To the modern ear this sounds like a peculiar mixture of activities for a business, but in the late 18th century these things were a normal part of an integrated printing business: notices of auction being placed in newspapers and adverts for the medicines being a staple of newspapers' advertising.

The Galeses had moved to Sheffield at a very exciting time: a time of change and ideas. The town grew rapidly as people moved in for work – from 9000 in 1736 to 40,000 in 1792, but was struggling economically. The American War of 1775 to 1783 and its aftermath and wars being declared by France, Spain and the Dutch in the late 70s caused trade to stagnate. Cost-cutting led to a demand for cheaper unskilled labour, outwith the traditional restrictive labour practices which came under the supposed control of the Cutlers' Company (an early trade association, possessing a regulatory role in law). There was discontent amongst the freemen cutlers against the Company who failed to act to stop labour being undercut as power concentrated in the hands of the merchant classes and large manufacturers, to the detriment of the "little mesters" and journeymen cutlers.

It was a town with very little aristocratic influence and no great civil power: its two magistrates in 1792 living out of town. Its many "little mesters" — highly skilled and well-paid craftsman — were often literate, and cherished their independence. Add to this Sheffield's "tavern-culture" – which provided spaces for reading newspapers aloud, debating and the singing of radical "educational" songs, such as those of Joseph Mather – a nursery for ideas.

The dissenting churches: Methodists, Presbyterians, Quakers, Baptists and Unitarians were strongly represented in the town, and were also no doubt important in their role in creating a seedbed for the formation of reform movements. These churches had a democratic basis: they got people used to the ideas of organising meetings, speaking for themselves and collecting subscriptions. E.P. Thompson quotes a historian from the 1820s: "Perhaps the manner in which Methodism has familiarized the lower classes to the work of combining in associations, making rules for their own governance, raising funds, and communicating from one part of the kingdom to another, may be reckoned among the incidental evils which have resulted from it…"

The ability to read was highly valued among dissenter households, especially because of the value they put on bible reading. They had a particular grievances resulting from the Test and Corporations Act, restricting their ability to hold certain official positions: this sense of exclusion and discrimination encouraged rather than inhibited independence of thought.

The people of the town in that era were described later by James Montgomery. He says: "they were then, as they are now, and I hope they ever will be, a reading and thinking people. According to the knowledge which they had, therefore, they judged for themselves on the questions of reform in parliament, liberty of speech, and of the press, the rights of man, and other egregious paradoxes, concerning which the wisest and best of men have always been divided, and never were more so than at the period above mentioned, when the decision, either way, was not to be merely speculative, but practical, and to affect permanently the condition of all classes of persons in the realm, from the monarch to the pauper…"

Following on from his reading of the Rev. Disney pamphlet, Gales looked for a church – the one they settled on was the Upper Chapel in Norfolk Street where the minister was Benjamin Naylor who had been educated at Warrington Academy where Joseph Priestley had been a tutor. There, Gales mixed with influential Sheffielders including Samuel Shore, who had been a part of Wyvill's Association – a group which petitioned for parliamentary reform, and which led to a motion in Parliament proposed by William Pitt in 1782, but which was lost by 161 to 141 votes. (Winifred said that Pitt's later volte-face showed: "how great, how mean, how versatile is Man." Other epithets were no doubt used in Sheffield's taverns.) Samuel Shore was also the brother-in-law of Thomas Walker, a Manchester cotton merchant, campaigner for Reform and radical printer.

Gales quickly established a sound reputation amongst the freemen cutlers by printing for them, and helping them with drafting notices and handbills. Jewitt said: "I fetched from his office the first job he had had in the town an advertisement for calling another general meeting and for some time afterwards a week elapsed without his having a job from the same employers." Winifred in her diary says that the employees were also "glad to find their grievances so moderately stated, and so respectfully submitted, and the printer was credited by both parties – the first for putting their demands into good language, and the latter for the propriety with which they were addressed." At this time Gales also published a folio family bible, made up of 60 sections at 6d each.

Winifred fell pregnant soon after their marriage, but the first child died after a few hours in March 1785, and this difficult birth almost killed Winifred as well. Their first surviving child, Joseph, was born on the 10th of April the following year. In amongst all this, Winifred somehow wrote her first novel, *The History of Lady Emma Melcombe and Her Family*, published in 1787.

Winifred was clearly a strong, spirited woman – that comes across from her writing and an understanding of the way she responded to events – how she dealt with the search of her house, with a mob that gathered outside, with her appearance before the magistrates, and her dealings with privateers (pirates) on the way to America etc. We can only speculate on just how involved she was in the editorial work of the newspaper, but it is reasonable to assume she was very hands-on, even if she could not be seen to be so. She was clearly involved in political discussions with visitors to their house – she was highly literate and ran the shop side of the business. Jewitt made this reference to her: "Mrs Gales a very clever woman being greatly considered as the editor on Gales leaving Sheffield." So, I think we must qualify our references to the editorial comments of Gales with a recognition that this may not be the work of a single person, and that Winifred's hidden hand might well have been behind some of the opinion pieces.

Sheffield had only one rather dated and old-fashioned newspaper at that time: *The Sheffield Advertiser*. It was stuck in its ways and out of tune with the populous, doing little more than reprinting the news from London Papers several days late without comment. It had next to no local news other than in notices paid for by advertisers.

Jewitt describes the Advertiser as "a stupid Tory Aristocratic thing, solely devoted to the 'Powers that Be' in which the Freemen and all that are now stigmatised as the 'lower orders' were unmercifully treated."

Circumstances were propitious for the founding of a new newspaper. It was a lawyer friend of Gales, Thomas Sambourne, who first suggested the idea of publishing a newspaper.

The Sheffield Register

The Galeses soon moved to a larger house on the other side of the Hartshead, the former home of Dr Buchan, from where their new venture of printing a weekly newspaper, *The Sheffield Register*, could be embarked upon.

Helping run the business were Joseph Gales' sisters. His sister, Anne (Nancy) had always lived with them according to Winifred, but they were also joined by Elizabeth and Sarah in running the household and business. Setting up a new newspaper required a significant initial investment: there were up-front costs that had to be paid before a single newspaper could be delivered: a duty of 3½d on every paper, 2/ stamps and duties on every advertisement, in addition to materials, and delivery costs. There was however a loophole for postage – if you got an MP to use their frank-mark, delivery was free. To this end, the support of William Wilberforce, MP for Yorkshire, was secured. An engraver named David Martin came in with the necessary capital investment, and became Gales' business partner in the venture.

The first page of the first edition of the *Register* prints an impressive if rhetorical and somewhat self-congratulatory introductory editorial:

"There is not perhaps any situation or profession amongst the mechanical part of mankind that is exposed to so much observation and censure as the printer of a newspaper. The various tastes that he has to please, the different opinions he has to combat and the trouble he must necessarily take, render it an arduous, difficult and expensive undertaking[...]

"The printer of a newspaper is entitled to some small share in the praise which is due to those who are serviceable to their species as his endeavours have tendency to promote trade and commerce, convey useful and desirable information and rescue from oblivion acts and events which would be lost to the world but for such registers and means of communication as the press furnishes and the industry of man avails himself of. A newspaper may be compared to a reservoir of water, for as the latter receives the beautiful springs of nature from all around it and distributes streams to supply the surrounding country so does the former receive its numerous articles of information from various sources, and, in its wide-extended circulation, furnishes the public with its agreeable and interesting contents. It makes known the wants and necessities of individuals and forms a link in the vast chain which connects mankind and each other. We see displayed in a mirror, the patriotism of one man, and the intrepidity of another, the magnanimity of a third and the generosity and humanity of a fourth, and thus discover perfection which exalts the species and stimulates us to follow their example, whilst on the other hand the artful villain, the bold and reprobate and all public pests of society are held before us as objects of abhorrence to be avoided and despised if we would escape from injury and ridicule."

Whatever its eventual achievements, the content of the newspaper over the first two years falls somewhat short of these idealistic, grandiloquent aspirations. Most of the paper was taken up with advertisements and recapitulation of national and European news culled from London papers. Editorial opinion in the first six months was infrequent and cautious. The proprietors of the newspaper appear to have been zealous to avoid giving offence and losing sales as they sought a viable level of circulation amongst what, at this stage, must have been a relatively prosperous commercial and professional clientele, whose values and politics were broadly reflective of their position in society though probably far from homogeneous given the high percentage of dissenters in the town and its surrounding area.

Local news 1787 - 1788

In the first year of the newspaper, local news was mainly a catalogue of marriages, deaths, crimes accidents and social events with a particular emphasis on musical performances.

Crime reports were mainly about burglaries, highway robbers and footpads, though from the beginning there are also stories of dishonest market traders. One of the first such is an account of the prosecution of a trader for selling rancid butter.

Accidents reported include a man killed when his millstone shattered and a Rawmarsh boy killed by a single blow from a thirteen-year-old following a dispute arising from a game of quoits. Reports of local social events include the "elegant dinner" enjoyed by the members of the Firework Club in honour of the King's birthday as well as the annual Cutlers' Feast, an event that still takes place in Sheffield.

Other local news included the success of a recent army recruiting drive in the town and a report on the recent improvements in the town, including new buildings, better regulation of markets and the extended range of manufactures.

In July the editor notes the "bright rays of increasing trade in the town with orders for Sheffield manufactured goods from Russia and other foreign parts," and, in August, editorial support is given for a newly founded organisation for recovering runaway apprentices. Editorial approval is also given to the relevant authorities for preserving the peace of the Sabbath by putting six boys in the stocks who were caught bathing in the river Don during church service.

In January of 1788, the newspaper notes a collection of £700 for the relief of the poor prompted by the recent spell of cold weather. In April, the Duke of Norfolk is commended for his £25 endowment of the newly erected Park Free School and in the same edition an anonymous individual is praised for donations to the two charity schools and to the welfare of inmates in the town gaol.

Also in April of that year, the editor comments that the behaviour and decorum of the girls at the charity school reflects well on the "regularity with which they are governed" and observes that in one year the girls have spun enough wool to make clothes for themselves and stockings for the boys at the boys charity school from the surplus. The school is commended for rescuing them from "indigence and perhaps vice."

Celebrations of the King's return to health included a ball and a firework display prompting the local Quakers to insert a notice in the paper giving thanks for the King's return to health but declining to participate in the illuminations, feasting and "riotous excess" – also expressing concern at the attacks on their property and persons occasioned by their abstention.

Other social events mentioned include "the brilliant and numerous assemblage of ladies" at the final subscription concert at the Assembly Rooms with the cessation of the concerts much regretted by the editor and an eulogy on the farewell performance of the celebrated actress Mrs Siddons in the play "Isabella or the Fatal Marriage" at Sheffield's theatre.

The July edition notes that a town meeting approved the proposals for erecting a new workhouse, though not without dissent, a subject to which *The Register* returns with some vigour the following year.

In December an editorial criticised the dangerous practise of "throwing fireworks, namely squibs, rockets and serpents popular at the time of the year." There are reports of a fire caused by someone throwing a squib on a stick through a house window and of two boys fined 20 shillings for throwing squibs.

❧

Editorial comment on national and foreign issues 1787-1788

The first comments on political issues appear in the autumn of 1787 where the editor remarks on the "perspicuity" of those involved in drafting the new American constitution and later adds: "we will now place America foremost in our history of the great ones of the earth," predicting that the "United Colonies of North America will hereafter emulate the most famous of past times."

An outspoken editorial in December argues for the abolition of the slave trade in trailing a petition that was expected to be placed before parliament. In it he says he hopes: "the time approaches in which Britons will shew themselves worthy the blessings they so amply share, by endeavouring to mitigate the unmerited sufferings of the persecuted Negroes." In another piece the editors welcome the fact that war with France over the Low Countries has been avoided with the following words:

"As inhabitants of so large, populous, and respectable a place as Sheffield whose manufactures in all probability would be affected by a stoppage of commercial intercourse between the rival nations, we sincerely rejoice that the cloud which has lately hung over our political hemisphere, is at length withdrawn, and the Sun of Peace again shines with renewed lustre."

Although these early editorial comments reflect the liberal values of the editors they were unlikely to alienate many customers or potential customers. If the paper had been printed and circulated in Bristol or Liverpool the comments on the Slave Trade would have been very controversial, but relatively few Sheffield businessmen would have had any substantial financial interest in the trade and those who did had publicly declared that they were prepared to abandon any such interest, according to the Yorkshire MP Wilberforce in a speech to the House of Commons the following year.

Editorial comment on political topics remained a rarity throughout the second year, 1788, as well. The commonest themes continued to be support of charitable action but the concern for the poor puts as much emphasis on encouraging morality as relief of hardship and suffering.

What little politics there was in the pages of the *Register* in the early days was confined to printing notices of the meetings of either side in the long rumbling dispute between the freemen cutlers and the Cutler's Company. Both sides took out adverts to put their own arguments – posturing that is reminiscent of the way those involved in trade disputes use the modern media.

One consistent cause supported by the newspaper both during and after this period in its history is the promotion of Sunday schools and charity schools. Sunday schools are valued far their moral instruction of children of the poor as well as for teaching children to read – the teaching of mathematics and writing was not thought appropriate on a Sunday.

As well as praise for the providers and regulators of these Sunday schools there is editorial censure for parents and masters of apprentices who prevent children attending. A church collection for the boys or girls charity schools always prompts praise for the amount collected and extols the excellence of the sermon – to provide due encouragement. In December he praises the generosity of "a few respectable manufacturers" in funding a new school to be built in Broad Lane and then promotes the idea that such schools should be built in all parts of the town.

Elsewhere Gales notes with approval a subscription to provide a dole distribution to 500 impoverished widows. In a later edition he praises the action of some leading business men in Manchester to encourage the "lower class of people" to pay stricter attention to their "religious and moral conduct" by, among other things, discouraging "shopkeepers from selling their wares and manufacturers working at their respective businesses on a Sunday."

The following is an interesting editorial published on August 2nd 1788, regarding the ruling by the House of Lords against the long established rights of the rural poor to glean (pick over leftover grain after harvest) – a further turning of the screw in favour off the rights of property, running alongside enclosure:

"The late decision of the judges respecting the right of gleaning, which the poor arrogate to themselves in the season which is now near at hand, militates against the sanction of Holy Writ, and the primitive feelings of benevolence which glowed in the breasts of our forefathers. It is true that the *right* was always the farmers to bestow, but custom from time immemorial, has established it almost independent of *asking leave*. The language of Boaz, and the

15

sentiments of the present owners of the 'golden grain' are not at all consonant. 'Let her glean even among the sheaves, and also let fall some of the handfuls on purpose for her, and leave them that she may glean them, and rebuke her not.' "

The biblical reference would come naturally to Gales, and the subject matter would have been of interest to many readers given that he had by then established a system of distributing the paper to many of the larger villages within a 40 miles radius of Sheffield.

One of the few editorials commenting on poverty without any accompanying moral exhortation or appeals to charity is in the December 13th edition where he reports that as a result of the recent great drought, mechanics of several [water driven] grinding wheels are employed only two hours per day with the consequence "that their families are reduced to great indigence."

❧❧

Correspondence and Advertisements 1787 - 1788

In the first year of publication, printed letters were infrequent, a marked contrast with the later years of the newspaper. Two letters were printed in support of charitable causes one on behalf of a charity for the relief of "decayed musicians and their families" and one arguing the case for the establishment of a free dispensary for the poor in the town. In September a letter was printed supporting the enclosure of common land on the grounds that this promoted improvements in agriculture and increased food production. This was a controversial issue in Sheffield among the poorer classes of society which prompted a near riot four years later, but the letter did not provoke anyone to write stating a contrary view. This too may be indicative of the class composition of readers of the newspaper in its first years.

If letters were infrequent in 1787, advertisements were abundant from the beginning and these must have been an important source of revenue for the printer. The adverts themselves provide interesting information about life in a provincial city at the time. Patent medicines were clearly popular and advertised remedies were offered for scurvy, rheumatic fever, gravel stones and griping of the bowels among other ailments. Services offered included tuition in horse riding, the supply of millstones and the effective prevention of bugs. The public is notified about the opening of a new tea warehouse and the services of a brazier and tin merchant and there is a request for information leading to the recovery of a brown mare "lost or stolen" in the neighbouring village of Attercliffe. There were notices of theatrical productions including Othello and Macbeth, and books advertised for sale included "A Key to Geography," "Select Stories for Sunday Schools" and a collection of farces recently performed at London theatres. Regular public notices included dates of stagecoach departures from Sheffield, shipping arrivals and departures at Hull and Gainsborough, and comparisons of the price of corn and other staples at Sheffield, Rotherham and Gainsborough Markets.

The content of advertisements did not change to any significant degree throughout the life of the newspaper. Taking two months in 1791 as another snapshot, there were advertisements for spring fashions, portrait painting, dancing lessons, fever drops and an "infallible" method of destroying rats and mice. Other advertisements were for recovery of runaway husbands [from the parish overseers], runaway apprentices and a missing "Spanish ass." Apprentices were sought by a penknife maker and a master baker, while another employer seeks a man to manage a steam engine who "must be thoroughly acquainted with the nature and workings of the engine." A metal refinery asks for the owner of a quantity of dirt found near Whiteley Woods containing two ounces of silver to the pound to come forward and claim ownership with proof that the pile of dirt belongs to the applicant.

Other correspondence in 1788 included a letter putting the case for the usefulness of banks, evidently not something about which there was universal consensus at the time. There is also a letter commenting on the decision of the Anglican bishops to restrict ordination of priests to university graduates and one which urges the establishment of "asylums" for discharged convicts where they can be gainfully employed.

In May, an editorial cites a correspondent who pokes fun at John Wesley for suggesting in a sermon at Bradford that the final day of God's Judgement and the end of the world would take place in 1836 – but that a new world of universal holiness and angelic purity would succeed it "because all the inhabitants would be Methodists!" This prompts correspondence including a letter from a self styled "Methodist" written in support of John Wesley and the "revival of pure Christianity" he had stimulated and also from Wesley himself, saying that he was just quoting from the Lutheran scholar Bengel, and that he had no opinion at all on when the millennial reign of Christ would begin – that he was only concerned with saving his own soul and those that hear him.

There is an interesting letter under the pseudonym "Asiaticus," presumably a correspondent of Asian extraction, commenting on the "rapacious avarice or caprice of an English tyrant or set of tyrants who have emerged from the bosom of obscurity to lord it over millions of their fellow creatures." This was presumably partly provoked by the trial, which started in 1788, of Warren Hastings, Governor of the East India Company, on charges of inciting massacres, extortion and torture – of which he was later acquitted.

Accounts of the trial hearings were published in the London news columns of *The Register*. This letter and two follow up pieces do not appear to have generated any correspondence rebutting the accusations. Perhaps few articulate Sheffield citizens were investors in the company.

Gales quotes the following letter in his editorial column, copied from a London paper:

"One whose afflictions may be supposed to speak very forcibly intreats the confectioners and gingerbread bakers who may read this paragraph, never more to use what is called by them frosting of cakes in order to shew their sweetmeats to greater advantage, and by this means tempt unwary children to slow, but certain destruction. The shining particles which they use for this purpose are nothing but minute particles of coloured glass whose terrible and destructive consequences deprived me of a little cherubim – A MOTHER"

He follows this by the following call for compliance with the law: "In our recollection there have been three similar ones within these four years. Let us entreat, in the most solemn manner, that it may at length have some substantial effect; and if it cannot be procured by an appeal to the feelings of those who *must* know what pernicious material they use, let them seriously take warning by reflecting, which is certainly truth, that their conduct is cognisable by the law, and that it would not be wonderful, should any disconsolate mother, like the above, take legal vengeance for the untimely end of a cherished offspring."

Poetry

Every edition devoted a part column to poetry under the heading "Repository of Genius" – an overstatement to say the least. Almost all the verse printed in 1787 was conventional in both style and subject including poems celebrating the King's birthday, a poem by a 15-year-old "young lady" on hearing the music of Handel and poems entitled "Disappointment in love," "To the muse of Ariosto" and "To the Redbreast."

In December, however, they printed a poem entitled reflections on the "Traffic of Negroes." Although the style and diction are conventional at least this addresses a deeply felt contemporary theme and is the first example of the Registers use of verse to complement issues raised in correspondence, news and editorial comment.

The first verse is as follows and the rest are in a similar vein:

Ah! Who are they across the seas
That guide the dark browed ship afar
Whose lips profess the God of Peace

Their deeds the ruthless God of war

Although much of the poetry in the later years of the newspaper continues to be on conventional subjects the proportion of verse on topical subjects increases, sometimes with a corresponding increase in quality.

Progress of the newspaper 1787 – 1788

From the beginning, the proprietors showed initiative in promoting the success and circulation of the paper at the expense of its rivals. In September they commissioned an express service from London which brought copies of the London papers to Sheffield ten hours earlier than the mail coach and this enabled them to incorporate London news in their weekly edition one day ahead of *The Sheffield Advertiser*. In October they publicised a delivery service to Manchester and thirty villages and towns within a twenty mile radius of Sheffield. A further editorial in January 1788 confirms the increase in circulation that had been achieved and issues an enhanced editorial manifesto:

"The proprietors of this newspaper, encouraged by its very encreased and extensive sale, take the liberty respectfully to inform the public, that they have, at a considerable expense, enlarged their source of intelligence, and laid out for such certain and authentic information as must infallibly prove the superiority of their paper to any other in the country. –At the same time that they are determined, with every proper degree of manly firmness and becoming spirit, to prosecute their intention of rendering *The Sheffield Register* an object of universal request, they take this opportunity also of declaring that, conscious of the rectitude of their measures, and determined to support that noble barrier of English liberty, the freedom of the press, all appeals, which are not either seditious or libellous, and signed by the parties, shall, by being paid for as advertisements, have insertion in their paper: and possessing these sentiments, which they are fully persuaded become them as men and Englishmen, they shall feel themselves perfectly at ease, as to what may be said of their conduct in a recent case, or any similar one. They know no party, nor will espouse any sentiments inimical to candour and truth. They beg leave to express their grateful thanks to the public, and to declare that no exertion shall be spared to merit the flattering encouragement they so warmly and so encreasingly experience."

This was bold undertaking and prompted one reader to write a letter welcoming the declaration and, with at least a hint of scepticism, expressing the hope that the intentions are translated into practice. However, it should be noted that such "appeals" expressed in correspondence had to be paid for, which limited contributions to those prosperous enough to make such payments – though it would appear likely that Gales relaxed this requirement in later years by publishing correspondence from readers who could not have had the means to pay.

❧

The Campaign far the Abolition of the Slave Trade

Between January and March 1788 the Register printed a flurry of correspondence about the abolition of slavery. This may have been partly set off by its December 1787 editorial and poem and accounts of parliamentary debates reported in the Register's extracts from the London news. The national campaign against the trade was gathering momentum. But the immediate trigger appears to be the report in the local news section in which it was stated that at "a numerous and respectable meeting of the principle inhabitants of the town and neighbourhood it was unanimously resolved to petition the House of Commons on behalf of those miserable inhabitants of Africa transported from their native country." If the view of the town meeting was unanimous the views expressed in the correspondence were not. The debate both inside, and presumably outside, the pages of the newspaper was polarised and sometimes heated, prompting one correspondent to write congratulating the editors for the stance they had taken in the face of strong criticism and urging them to continue.

In April 1788 the editor praised Wilberforce for his four-hour speech presenting the Sheffield petition to parliament predicting with some foresight that "posterity will reverence him as the active friend of humanity."

It was a subject he returned to from time to time when the opportunity occurred. For example, in support of the boycott of West Indian sugar and rum in 1791, he printed an anecdote of cruel treatment on a slave trade ship. He refers to the perversion of wit and ingenuity entailed by attempts to laugh at a laudable purpose such as abolition of the slave trade. "The most pitiful thing we have lately seen, appeared in the London papers of last week, in the form of a petition from the 'Ourang Outangs, Jackoos[1] and other next of kin of the African Negroes,' attempting to prove them of the same species; and under the appearance of admiration, ridiculing the favourers of abolition. Surely this unfortunate race is sufficiently degraded by being the objects of an iniquitous traffic, without being in every degree levelled with the beasts that perish." He compares it to the speech of Shylock: "Hath not a Jew hands…" substituting the word Jew for African.

⚒

The Running of the Business

On March 27th 1788 the partnership between Gales and Martin was dissolved. From this date Gales was sole proprietor and editor of the newspaper. The Register gave notice of the dissolution but Gales only comment was to thank the subscribers for their support

---

[1] General Jackoo was a performing monkey from the French court who was dressed in human clothing and made to perform tricks such as riding horses

and to express a hope that this would continue. No reason was given. It has been suggested that the dissolution may have been prompted by political differences but this seems unlikely. In its first two years, both before and after the partnership was dissolved, the newspaper's stance on political issues was moderate and consistent with the views of most of the business and professional classes in the town. Martin as well as Gales was pro-reform in his political orientation, and is named as one of the founders of the later Sheffield Society for Constitutional Reform. It may have been little more than Martin was a sleeping partner and Gales had paid off the loans.

❧❧

The Centenary of the Glorious Revolution

In November 1788 Sheffield in common with most other English towns celebrated the centenary of the "Glorious Revolution" – the accession of William III to the throne of England and the passing of the Bill of Rights with his agreement the following year. This bill, which became known as the English Constitution, restricted the powers of the king, among other things, by removing his right to suspend laws approved by parliament, levy taxes or initiate foreign wars without the agreement of parliament, or to interfere unduly with the election of parliament. Religious toleration was also granted to Protestant dissenters – the right to worship as they chose.

Gales in an editorial wrote: "from this glorious period the animating breath of Liberty has diffused peace and increased commerce among the subjects of Britain." *The Register* also printed a poem entitled "Ode to the Revolution" and describes the public meeting and celebrations in Sheffield. A musical event followed a sermon by the Reverend Wilkinson vicar of Sheffield "taking advantage of Sheffield having the greatest number of good chorus singers than any other [town] excepting the metropolis."

Wilkinson's sermon received such acclaim from many of his audience that they wanted to print and distribute it. Wilkinson declined saying it was a hasty composition not worthy of preservation for posterity. As one of the two town magistrates he may have thought it politic that some of his spontaneously expressed views were not recorded in print.

The public meeting was followed by a dinner at the largest tavern in town: the Tontine Inn, the main stage coach inn, built in 1783. (It occupied the whole of the site now taken up by Wilkinsons on Haymarket). Gales printed the full list of toasts proposed. They make interesting reading and one can readily imagine that there was some rivalry and game playing in the toasts proposed in succession by those of conservative and reformist persuasion attending the dinner. No doubt the toasts to the Glorious Revolution, King William III and the "patriots" who supported him received general acclaim. But the toasts to the continuation of trial by jury, freedom of the press, habeas corpus and the "cause of liberty throughout the globe" may have prompted toasts to the Queen and Royal family, the Duke of Norfolk and to his eldest son by way of repartee. Whether or not there was such a divergence of inebriated enthusiasms, it is an undoubted fact that a number of the aspirations and freedoms subject of these toasts were curtailed or ignored in the period of repression which began only four years later, events which *The Sheffield Register* records with candour and detail. Many of the more liberal prominent citizens who attended the dinner appear to have lost the will to support these institutions and values when the repression began.

Correspondence 1789

In 1789 there are letters criticising the practice of duelling and the increasingly popular sport of boxing. There is a letter from a Scot taking exception to some of Dr Samuel Johnson's remarks about his native country and another deploring the miserable version of psalms sung in local churches. A philanthropic correspondent proposes the establishment of a fund to provide inoculations for the poor occasioned by an outbreak of smallpox in the town. At the end of the year there is the first of a series of letters from a correspondent in Mansfield setting out his views on education arguing the case for schools to teach more mathematics and science to prepare men for careers in industry and commerce and criticising grammar schools for being "seminaries" which do no more than prepare pupils for entry to universities.

The subject matter of this correspondence is an interesting indicator of the contemporary issues which moved readers of the newspaper to seek to influence their fellow citizens but other than the slave trade and a continuing concern with philanthropic causes and matters relating to religion, common themes are hard to identify at this stage in the life of the newspaper.

There is, however, an interesting exchange of correspondence between "A Votary of Freedom" and "A Friend to Freedom" on the dispute between the Cutler's Company and the freemen cutlers. It is a classic free-trade argument. "Votary" argues for the removal of restrictions on trade such as limits on apprentices and outsiders coming into the trade: "Do away with the clog, and we shall have money and genius flow into the town; the trade will be pushed with ten times the vigour it ever yet experienced to all parts of the globe, freedom will erect her god-like standard among us…" "Commerce should be unconfined – should be free as the air we breathe."

"Friend" replies with concerns for employment and wages, and for being driven towards child labour as in Manchester or Birmingham, as labour rates are driven down, unregulated. He believes that he called himself "A Votary of Freedom by mistake when he undoubtedly meant, that of slavery." "Does he not act like the chief captain of a desperate gang of highway men? Or like a pirate who has discovered a large booty, and summons up all his strength to attack and take it away from the rightful owners? Does he not say as much as that his gang has signed the Corporation's [the Cutlers' Company] death warrant?"

The Campaign for a New Sheffield Workhouse

In July 1788 *The Register* reported that a town meeting had approved proposals for a new workhouse, the workhouse at West Bar being some sixty or so years old, and inadequate. There was no clear consensus on the proposals and progress appears to have been slow as a result. Gales returned to the subject in August 1790 in an impassioned and powerful editorial. The opening paragraphs are as follows:

> "Is it consistent with the principles of humanity that the poor should be crowded together in close rooms of three or four yards square, and three or four persons obliged to lie in the same bed?
>
> "Is it consistent with these principles that there should not be sufficient discrimination of age or character in the treatment of the poor; that the repose of age should be disturbed by the unfeeling gaiety of youth, and that the virtuous matron should be compelled to associate in the same room and sometimes partner the same bed, with the abandoned prostitute? Is it consistent with these principles, that aged couples who have lived in credit and esteem, perhaps contributed through a long life to the maintenance of the poor by the labour of their hands, and are at length driven by age and misfortune to the workhouse, should be forced to associate with the most abandoned persons, enjoy no intervals of tranquillity for conversing with their God, and that their last hours which ought to be dedicated to retirement, and the great interests of the eternal world, should be interrupted by noise and clamour, and embittered by a sense of that unhappy situation in which they are compelled to endure such aggravated affliction? Is it consistent with these principles that there should be no rooms appointed for the sick, and those who labour under noisome and offensive complaints, and who for the sake of others as well as themselves, ought to be separated from the rest of the poor?"

Other questions address the absence of education and instruction for children both resident in the workhouse itself and supported outside in the community, the adverse consequences of boarding out children with people who don't want them, the inappropriate accommodation for the temporarily unemployed and wives of soldiers on active service abroad, the lack of supervision, and the inadequacy of the one small workroom. The editorial concludes by arguing that an extension of the current building could not meet the need and that the only effective and humane solution would be a new and larger building on a new site funded by a loan. He urges the people of the town not to abandon the resolution "expressed almost unanimously at the previous meeting," implicitly acknowledging that opposition has been mounting and support needs to be bolstered.

The committee set up to prepare proposals, chaired by James Wilkinson, Vicar of Sheffield, finally reported in December, and in a further editorial Gales urges acceptance of proposals "founded on real necessity… in which the virtuous instruction and industrious employment of the poor are as much objects of regard as their comfort and proper accommodation," and pointing out that the size of the building proposed was only sufficient for immediate needs but the site large enough for a future extension if this be required.

No immediate decision was taken and in 1790 Gales returns to the issue with reports and correspondence about the Shrewsbury workhouse which was operating on a model similar to that proposed for Sheffield with the aim of convincing people that extending the opportunities for in-house employment would not damage business interests in the town.

On April 8th 1790 the proposals for a new workhouse, on a site between Broad Lane and Trippet Lane, were rejected at public meeting prompting Gales to observe: "The spirit of philanthropy never received a greater check." He criticises opponents of the plan for their discourtesy to the Reverend Wilkinson who chaired the meeting and deplores the unsatisfactory progress. At the time there was no formal system for electing local representatives who could make decisions on such matters and consequently these decisions were taken at public meetings. Gales complains that when philanthropic schemes are first proposed few attend – a resolution is passed to set up a committee to prepare a plan and after much hard work has been expended those whose only interest is to protect their own financial interests pack the meeting and vote it down.

Over the next two months correspondents continue to address the issue, one of whom seeks to moderate between the opposing factions while another categorically opposes the alternative proposals to extend the existing workhouse on the grounds of the total unsuitability of the building. Further editorials urge the town's inhabitants to find a solution. But it appears that the divisions and the heightened feelings they generated were too great to be bridged and there was no formal mechanism for resolving differences.

The old workhouse was finally pulled down in 1829 and then replaced, not by a purpose built building, but by a converted former silk and cotton mill in what is now Russell Street at Kelham Island.

◦ৠৡ৹

The Campaign to Build the Sheffield Infirmary

In April 1788 Gales had reported on the annual meeting of the governors of Nottingham Infirmary and added the following editorial comment:

> "It is with the highest regret we consider Sheffield as almost the only large manufacturing town in the kingdom that cannot boast one of these noble and charitable institutions – especially when we consider the trade of Sheffield exposes the mechanics to more frequent accidents than most other manufacturers are liable to; and from its populousness and number of working inhabitants, distressed sicknesses cannot be less in number than in any other large town. Spirit and liberality in a benevolent cause are never wanting among the gentlemen of Sheffield and the neighbourhood; we wish and hope, therefore, that a future day will remedy this apparent defect."

At some point in the next three years a committee was set up to promote and develop such a project and when a public appeal was launched in 1792 Gales used the newspaper to promote and assist the project. The names of subscribers to the appeal were published and praised for their generosity. Money was received from people of all ranks. In April the newspaper announces that the Duke of Norfolk donated £3500 and there was probably little surprise when the following week Earl Fitzwilliam, the county Lord Lieutenant, subsequently donated the same sum. Later the list of subscribers includes a collective donation from the grinders of Intake Holme Wheel and the workmen at a silver-plating workshop. He reports that there was so much enthusiasm for the project among the working people that donations were offered from the administrators of sick clubs though these were declined on the grounds that the funds were 'sacred' to the original purpose for which they had been collected.

In September he reported that a site had been agreed for the Infirmary, and in September the following year he recorded the ceremonial laying of the first stone and the commencement of building on what was then Walkley Road, now Infirmary Road (though the Infirmary closed in the 1980s and was converted to offices).

The success of this campaign in contrast to the campaign for the new workhouse is interesting. The cause of the sick probably had more appeal to the philanthropist than the cause of the able bodied poor, even though these were probably in a minority among the workhouse residents. But the principal difference is likely to be the fact that the finance was obtained by voluntary donation not any an ongoing levy and the section of the population whose main concern was defending their financial interest did not need to contribute, and the amount they contributed, if anything, was under their own control. Although the appeal was launched at a public meeting there was no recorded dissent and the only resolutions concerned the questions of managing the fund, raising and planning the project, not the principle of whether the infirmary should be built.

The French People Burst the Bonds of Tyranny

On July 11th 1789 Gales reports that "commotions" in France "have come to a crisis, greater, more sudden, and more fortunate than expected" with the establishment of the National Assembly – a lesson to nations to watch with a jealous eye the increase of the personal wealth, influence, and authority of their sovereigns."

On July 25th the paper reports on the storming of the Bastille, and that "several other violent excesses have been committed." The governor and commandant of the garrison were "conducted to the Place de Grieve – the place of public execution – where they beheaded them, stuck their heads on tent poles and carried them in triumph to the Palais Royal, and through the streets of Paris." The French Revolution proper had begun. From this point on, events in France and consequential events in surrounding countries receive regular coverage in the newspaper, in news columns, correspondence and intermittent editorial comment.

In Sheffield, the events in France progressively divided public opinion as was the case in the rest of the country. For the first two years of his newspaper's existence Gales can be said to have more or less maintained his initial declared editorial policy to "know no party." In terms of formal political parties this continued to be the case but increasingly the newspaper's stance became one of overt support for libertarian movements abroad and reform of parliament at home. Although he continues to consistently condemn violence and attacks on property, on other issues the newspaper's stance in editorials, extracts from various writers and even correspondence is preponderantly in favour of the changes and reforms taking place in revolutionary France and adjacent countries. Over the previous three months Gales had incorporated a weekly letter from "a friend in London" into his regular column which incorporated editorial comment and local news. On August 1st this letter from "the Printer's friend" contains the following observations on events in France:

> "The kingdom of France cannot be modelled by ours, nor do the people, by the way they are going to work, seem as if they

would obtain a redress of their grievances. The original party, who had digested their mode of a reform, had justice clearly on their side, and exhibited a specimen of manly consistency which is not to be found in the history of nations. The people, however poor, desperate, and beyond control, are converting that to an evil, which with by moderation they might have counted on as their only hopes of happiness. Numbers indiscriminately pour in from every quarter, and the promiscuous mixture of the dregs of the people with the respectable burgeois,(sic) mocks at every effort of subordination. Le Marquis de la Fayette, their idol, with tears, vainly explores a relaxation of their unadvised and impolitic fury – every obnoxious object is put to the death by the mob..."

This contrasts sharply with Gales own comment on these events "To do the French justice they have struggled most nobly for liberty and their acts have been directed by moderation and firmness" and he continues by referring to the "small number of lives in such a monumental struggle." He adds: "The sceptre will remain in the royal hands but directed by the public voice concentrated in their freely chosen representatives." In other words at this stage he predicts that they will adopt something similar to the English constitutional model. The weekly contribution from the "Printer's friend in London" was henceforth discontinued.

Over the next months *The Register* summarises the debates in the French National Assembly on the content and wording of the proposed Declaration of Rights and problems in raising finance and supplying Paris with food. In August he reports the burning of over 500 provincial residences of French noblemen and refers to the riots in Cherbourg adding the comment: "The state of the nation is a severe lesson to King and people and I hope to see arise from our present confusion that happy state of society, subordination with out slavery." A report on alleged events in the Franche Comté region describes how a seigneur invited local people who welcomed the revolution to a celebration, then blew them up with gunpowder, killing many and there is also a feature article on the hardship of life in the Bastille. Another story recounts the deeds of a 17-year-old young woman, described as a contemporary Joan of Arc in stopping a horse driven cart, taking wheat out of Paris where there were serious food shortages at the time.

In September Gales observes that events in France are spilling over into neighbouring states with popular demonstrations in Liege in support of magistrates being elected by the people not by the Prince Bishop and an uprising in Belgium against the rule of the Austrian Emperor. He cannot resist embellishing the events with the customary rhetorical flourish. "The French revolution like planets of a superior order will be attended by many satellites."

On October 21st he prints the following extravagantly partisan letter "from a gentleman in Brussels to a friend in the town" – probably one of the earliest examples of a front-line war correspondent writing for an English provincial newspaper:

"I have been here some weeks, but leave tomorrow. The emperor, whom Mirabeau justly styles Bourrean Couronne[2] (The Crown of Cruelty) is exercising at this moment a tyranny in Brussels unexampled in the history of the last two centuries. The supposed discovery of a conspiracy is the pretext for severity. Forty persons – whose sole crime has been a correspondence with the absentees from Brussels (who could not bear the tyranny of Joseph *[Joseph II of Austria]* any longer) and an attempt to support those privileges which he has despotically wrenched from them, by absolving himself from the obligations in his installation oath, and by suppressing the states of Brabant, – are now in confinement. Some have been tried; and Monday next is appointed to shed the blood of these martyrs. Bodies of armed soldiers are searching every house in Brussels this day, and stealing from the inhabitants every weapon which a cruel and timid policy fears may be raised against it. They have profaned the sanctuaries of religion; they have sequestered all the abbeys, they have ransacked the cells of monks and invaded the retirement of nuns; they have forged a story that

---

[2] Actually it was: Bourreau Couronné (crowned executioner)

32

in the English convent a large quantity of cartridges and fuses was discovered. The patriots are assembled at the frontiers to the number of 40,000. An attack by them upon Brussels, and an insurrection to support them within is every moment expected. – If the delay is four days all will be lost! Seven thousand men are upon the march to reinforce the garrison."

A letter on December 12th contains a hyperbolic eulogy to the revolution taken from an article in the London based Analytic Review. "The sun of freedom has risen and the mists of despotism will vanish before the brightness of his rays."

Gales own end of the year editorial reviewing political developments in Europe in 1789 is sober by comparison, noting that in France liberty has succeeded an arbitrary monarchical power, and the emancipation of the Netherlands from Imperial power while Britain "enjoys the blessings of peace and the increase in commerce rising above the dubious situation of the nations of Europe."

❧❧❧

The Campaign to End Discrimination Against Protestant Dissenters.

For over 100 years laws had been in force in England forbidding dissenters from holding any civil or military office, restricting them from obtaining patents, entering universities or obtaining employment a lawyers or schoolteachers. These laws were set out in the Test and Corporation Acts: the "test" being whether the individual partook of holy communion in the established church at least once every six months. Parliament rejected a petition to repeal these laws in 1787 and over the next three years a national campaign was mounted to bring the matter back to parliament in order that such a repeal could be enacted.

In December 1789 Gales published an editorial in *The Sheffield Register* supporting the case for repealing these acts and ending the discrimination "finding it remarkable that they are still supported by people who avow themselves as friends of religious and civil liberty" and quoting the English philosopher Joseph Locke: "It is narrowness of spirit that has been the cause of our miseries and confusions. Absolute liberty, just and true liberty, equal and impartial liberty is the thing we stand most in need of."

This was followed over the next six weeks by a series of lengthy factual articles setting out the detailed working of these acts, and quotations supporting the campaign, from eminent contemporary dissenters such as the prominent Birmingham chemistry pioneer Joseph Priestley. The coverage of the issue prompted a letter from the Church of England clergy in Leeds in defence of the status quo which Gales true to his declared editorial policy printed in full and a response to this letter from clergy belonging to dissenter chapels in the same town.

The issue came to parliament in March 1790. *The Register* gives several columns to the speech by Fox proposing the repeal, half a column to the reply by Pitt opposing the repeal and only a three line mention to the other key opposing speech by Edmund Burke – hardly impartial coverage. The vote was lost by 294 to 105 votes and the discriminatory acts remained in force until 1828.

On June 25th 1790 *The Register* contains a brief report of Joseph Priestley's complaint that a dissenter friend nominated by himself and three other distinguished members was rejected by the Royal Society despite his knowledge of both chemistry and philosophy being exceptional and greater than his own. In the following edition Gales quotes from an actual or fictitious correspondent:

> "A correspondent wonders that Dr Priestley should be
> offended because his friend was not admitted as a member of
> the Royal Society; and that he should ascribe this
> disappointment to 'party manoeuvres,' occasioned 'by
> religious or political' disputations. The Doctor has surely
> forgotten that his friend was a dissenter, and himself an
> heretic of the first magnitude, who has written against
> Bishops and dignitaries, eminent for zeal and orthodoxy.
> Now as many of these exalted personages are members of the

society in question, the Doctor might easily have foreseen, that they would feel no great inclination to associate with heretics and sectaries – more especially in with those among them, from whom they had received literary assaults – in return for the most unexampled meekness and condescension. It would not surprise me (says our correspondent) if this rash unfounded charge of Dr. P should dispose the above mentioned venerable corps to move for the exclusion of all the dissenters from the Society; or to make an application to Parliament for a law to compel them to qualify, as the Test Act already requires all officers in government employ, by partaking of the holy communion. Every reason or argument which can be advanced to prove that dissenters should be deprived of civil honours, will be equally strong against their being admitted to philosophical honours. Nay more so, for certainly the Astronomer-royal is a more respectable and consequential personage than the Ratcatcher-royal!"

It is likely that the sardonic tone and the heavy irony are a product of despair about the possibility of achieving justice on such issues through parliamentary process. Gales and other dissenters were strengthened in their belief that little if any redress of grievances could be obtained from such an unrepresentative and unreformed parliament, and that political campaigning should be focussed on the reform of Parliament itself as the key to redress of all such grievances. This is made explicit at a later stage when he commits *The Register* wholeheartedly to supporting the cause of parliamentary reform.

Cruelty to Animals

This is another issue on which Gales used the newspaper to attempt to mould public opinion. In July 1790 he urges parishes to stop the practices of bull baiting, bear baiting and cock fighting at the annual "feasts" which were due to take place in many surrounding villages. On August 20th he claims some success, in that bull and bear baiting had been banned at a number of such feasts, an exception being Swinton where there were nevertheless strong protests from a number of parish residents. A correspondent who signs himself as "a Parish Officer" from an unnamed village near Barnsley writes that the practice is still more widespread than Gales is suggesting and partly blames the local clergy for being insufficiently active in promoting the suppression of these practices.

In a later edition Gales returns to the issue of bear baiting with an account of a bystander being seriously injured by a goaded bear becoming out of control, this time stressing the public safety argument rather than the humanitarian argument. Later still, in 1793 he returns to the issue of "bear and bull baiting, cock-fighting and throwing at cocks." He welcomes the decline in practices which sacrifice innocent victims at the "shrines of idleness and intemperance," but urges constables and overseers in surrounding villages to prevent "any repetitions of this national disgrace – parents and masters would also do well to caution their children and apprentices against such horrid amusements, which tend to debase the mind [...] thus rendering it "callous to the softer feelings of humanity, and fit it for deeds without a name."

Elsewhere he condemns the practice of hare coursing with dogs, citing a recent event where a pregnant female hare was killed as well as another which was caring for young as "acts of absolute barbarity." On all these issues his aim appears to have been one of stimulating local action to achieve suppression, not one of promoting parliamentary legislation.

At the approach of Shrove Tuesday he addresses the practice of throwing at cocks: where a cockerel was tied to a stake and killed by stones being thrown at it. It is not just the cruelty to: "a creature which is more universally useful to man than any of the feathered race... a creature whose voice, like a trumpet summoneth man to his labour in the morning..." "a weak, defenceless animal; an animal however brave by nature, and courageous even to death against his equal." It is also the dehumanising effect on the perpetrators that concern Gales: "an habit of cruelty which may end in murder" –

caused by the behaviour of parents who neglect to instruct their children in the duty of mercy to brutes" "by not restraining their children in time from wanton cruelty to birds and insects" which shuts their ears and hardens "their hearts against the cries of suffering animals, renders them deaf also to the cries of nature…"

This dislike of violence extended to other sports indulged in:

"Two young heroes of the *smithy*, *hammered* each other, on Crooksmoor, for a trifling wager, on Monday morning – to the great *edification* and *entertainment* of many hundreds of spectators – for *an hour and twenty minutes*, when the battle was *drawn*, by consent. One of the combatants is likely to lose an *eye*. – The other had only *one*."

Other Local News and Comment 1790

The Register's weekly editorial continues to furnish a modern reader with interesting, often curious, and sometimes shocking, snapshots into the life of the times.

On February 5th he recounts a story – reminiscent of the beginning of *The Mayor of Casterbridge* – of a young woman deserted by her husband, sold for two shillings at Burton fair by the parish overseers to whom she had applied for poor relief. She was delivered to her purchaser in a halter. Gales comments: "Such is too frequently the practice of our parish overseers."

The following week he reports that in Sheffield five men were put in the stocks for tippling in a public house during divine service on a Sunday and two boys were also made to do penance in church for playing "tip" during service hours. (This is probably the game later called "knurr and spell" where a shaped piece of wood is tipped up with a bat, sending it spinning into the air where it has to be struck as far as possible.) In the same month he warns the public about a group of "young villains," aged 15 to 16 infesting the Castle Street area, thieving from residents and shopkeepers.

An important event that year was the execution in April of John Stevens and Thomas Lastley (an event also marked by a song by Joseph Mather, a filesmith balladeer of the time). Their execution served to raise people's sense of injustice, in particular against the local magistrates. It followed what was believed to be little more than a Saturday night, post-tavern prank gone wrong the previous Autumn. Along with two others Stevens and Lastley ran off with a basket containing a shoulder of mutton and a few groceries from a fellow workman named Wharton, with whom they had been drinking. They took it to a pub and had the mutton cooked. They thought Wharton would follow them, since they had told him where they were going, and had collected money between them to pay for the meat. Angered at the prank, however, Wharton had gone to the constable, and the four were arrested for highway robbery and they were committed to the assizes.

The arrests coincided with a visit by the Prince of Wales and the Duke of Norfolk to Wentworth Woodhouse, the home of the nearest local aristocrat, Earl Fitzwilliam. Was the magistrate, Wilkinson, who was not particularly known for being a harsh man, trying to show he was in control of the town in advance of his invitation to the ball in the Prince's honour? Lastley and Stevens went to the gallows. Petitions to London were made but a reprieve did not arrive until two days later. There was anger in the town when the news arrived, directed at Wharton who was believed to have exaggerated the story for the sake of £100 "blood money" (the practice of giving money to those providing evidence leading to a capital sentence). *The Register* reports the ensuing scenes:

> "The behaviour of these unhappy men since their condemnation, manifested a hearty contrition for their crimes, and a becoming resignation to their ignominious fate [...] Much disturbance has arisen in this town since the execution[...] from an idea that the prosecutor swore to aggravated circumstances, which really did not happen. This suspicion has gathered strength from the solemn asseverations of the two unfortunate men, communicated by a letter to their shopmates, dated the evening preceding their execution – The populace have several times beset Wharton's house, and hung the figure of a man on a gibbet before his door; but yesterday they were so violent as to break every

window, and otherwise so much damage his house, as to render it scarcely habitable. – The current report, when our paper went to press was, that Wharton had escaped in woman's cloaths."

In May the story of the month is the arrival of the first delivery of fresh fish in Sheffield Market from a new source providing greater quantities of cod, haddock whiting and skate of superior quality and at a lower price than previously. Apparently, the event was welcomed by all except local butchers and poulterers. There is also a story of a dishonest baker who seeing the weights and measures inspectors coming inserted half crowns in his loaves to bring the weight up to standard. A passer by observing this went into the shop and purchased all the loaves in the presence of the inspectors. Dishonest traders are a favourite target in the column.

In June there is an account of celebrations in the town of Chesterfield over the birth of an heir to the Duke of Devonshire, whose country seat Chatsworth is a few miles from the town, and in August he notes the start of "moor game shooting" in the area then as now on the 12th of August – a date set in law even back then to preserve game for the land-owning classes.

That there is not huge coverage of political events is evidenced by the scant mention of the dispute between the scissor manufacturers and their grinders that began in late Spring of 1790. Jonathan Watkinson, a master scissor smith, announced that he was changing the terms on which he contracted out grinding – effectively a pay cut. The long-accepted tradition was for fourteen blades to be sent out and, accepting that sometimes one or two were substandard, the expectation was for only twelve to be returned and paid for. This also allowed some leeway for "perks of the trade" – any that weren't broken being sold on. (See also the songs by Joseph Mather, *Watkinson and his Thirteens,* and *The Hallamshire Haman*).

The strike is briefly mentioned on August 17th when there is a short statement of the facts, the only comment being that the dispute is "likely to be attended by serious consequences." According to the newspaper, "The scissor manufactory, from this stoppage in the grinding, is nearly at a stand." He reports on a meeting the night before of the manufacturers and their decision to raise a subscription of several hundred pounds to "prosecute a certain number of persons who they suppose have been principals in the scheme of turning out to effect an advance in wages."

The outcome follows five weeks later. Five of the leaders of the scissor grinders' strike were imprisoned in Wakefield for: "having kept goods from their employers, in an unfinished state, *eight days*, and refusing to *finish* them." Gales comments: " It would give us great pleasure to announce an end being put to the disputes betwixt the grinders and manufacturers, with respect to wages: many of both, we apprehend, are much distressed on account of them; the former, for *money* --- the latter, for *labour*."

An early foray into the debate on parliamentary reform comes by way of the printing of a letter setting out a list of the 61 "rotten boroughs" – parliamentary seats sending, in most cases, two members to the house, all on the votes of fewer than 40 men of property, some having only one or two electors. (This compared to Sheffield's 40,000 plus, without a single representative.)

In October he promotes a book of engravings by his former partner, David Martin, lamenting the fact that visitors to the "sable" (i.e. black) town rarely visit or praise its beautiful surroundings, a theme echoed by many other local writers over the next 200 years.

❧

Humanity's Greatest Victory Over Prejudice – France 1790

Reports on what was happening in France and neighbouring countries continue through 1790 with a focus increasingly placed on those events which the editor thought could or should have implications for Britain.

Throughout the first half of the year he reports on debates and decisions of the French National Assembly, drawing attention to those that advance the cause of liberty and equality further than in Britain. In January he reports the decision to extend full "political and civil rights of citizens to men of all persuasions, Christians, Mahomedons or Hindoos, in France." The decree of the Assembly was that: "non-Catholics shall be capable of all employments, civil and military, as other citizens." Next to this, on the front page, to make a strong statement, are details of a meeting in Wakefield of "a very numerous and respectable meeting of protestant dissenting ministers and lay deputies from congregations of the three denominations in the West Riding of the County of York, and of other gentlemen, friends to the application to parliament for the repeal of the Corporation and Test Acts…" The resolutions of the meeting are printed in full alongside the report from Paris – the message couldn't be clearer.

In July he reports and comments on the Assembly's decision to abolish all titles, liveries and coats of arms and their declaration that "heredity nobility cannot subsist in a free state." Gales comments approvingly, abandoning his customary caution: "The decree of the French National Assembly to abolish all distinctions amongst the people, is perhaps as great a victory over prejudice as human nature can attain. Actions, not names, ennoble mankind; a virtuous character derives no additional lustre from the adventitious aid of a Title." There were few people with titles in Sheffield and perhaps such remarks were not likely to alienate many of his customers but they would inevitably have contributed to him incurring the enmity of the aristocratic party so influential on the national scene.

In the last three months of the year the emphasis changes. There are reports of mutinies in the French army suppressed with much loss of life, problems in ensuring adequate food supplies for the Parisian poor, mob violence on the streets and sacking of aristocratic houses. There are divisions between the king and the Assembly with both sides arming themselves. The loyalty of the regular army to the Assembly is questioned. It was in this context that Edmund Burke wrote his famous letter condemning the French Revolution and implicitly encouraging the British government to promote counter-revolution. *The Register* prints a brief summary of Burke's letter but initially avoids directly challenging Burke's views on France, though questioning his criticisms of the London Constitutional Societies and defending the reasonableness of their guiding principles.

At this stage most of his direct comments on events in France are non-committal. On this and other issues his natural caution led him to reflect on events before coming to a judgement. He writes that France's "present state, views and probable fate elude the reasonings and even the conjectures of the wisest statesmen." And later: "Of France in her present situation little can be said, for who can analyse chaos or foresee how afterwards its materials will be arranged."

However, at the turn of the year in his review of politics he no longer equivocates. After observing on the dramatic changes in France that have "for two years astonished and fixed the attention of Europe" he turns his attention to Burke and his allies in a thinly veiled attack. In Gales' opinion, the revolution in France is fixed and not to be subverted:

> "To the reasoning of those ingenious and distinguished persons who labour to discredit the nature, and decry the stability of the French government, we oppose the common opinion of men of plain, though not much cultivated, understanding. It is paradoxical, but not perhaps, wholly untrue, that the brightest men are often the greatest fools. Fine imaginations and lively positions, and consequently prejudices, are not uncommonly found in conjunction: men of extensive knowledge, their minds stored with analogies ad infinitum, find a plausible theory for the support of any doctrine they consider, or wish to be considered as true. But when the understanding thus enlists in the service of the will, splendour of genius, instead of a lamp of light, becomes an *ignus fatuus* that leads into error. We would rather follow the authority of the people, than those that pretend to be doctors of the people."

He continues by positing that the revolution in France will be permanent on the grounds that a counter-revolution cannot succeed "because the great mass of the people are enthusiasts in the cause of freedom." Nor could an invasion suppress the revolution and restore the monarchy because, though limited victories could be initially achieved by invading armies, especially naval victories, ultimate military success is not possible in an invasion of a large populous country like France: " to subdue the people is not within the compass of the English, Savoyards, Spaniards, and Austrians united." And besides, the expense and logistics of maintaining long supply lines over time could not be sustained and the perseverance of invading armies would be eroded.

The Wakening of the Slumbering Giant

After describing the "level path" of private life in her reminiscences, Winifred goes on to describe the "rough path" of political discordance. This was a subject which, "after slumbering for many years, awoke like a giant refreshed with wine, and became a subject of great interest to all ranks and parties."

"The people agitated, and alarmed, saw only Tyranny and Oppression on one hand, and Reform on the other – the rulers would see nothing but Rebellion, and Revolution! To men capable of thinking, neutrality of opinion was impossible and if their thoughts ever passed into speech, or became visible on paper, they were ranked either as royalists or disorganisers, for the government party ranked all in the latter class who presumed to advocate the rights of the people. The former comprised all those, with some honourable exceptions, whose hereditary possessions, or official situations rendered it in their interests to keep things as they were. Their slogan was *aris et focis* which translated according to their views would have been "our places – our pensions." Our right to trample upon the poor rogues who want to reform us! The timid, the selfish, the bigoted of all classes ranked on their side. To this formidable phalanx was added those innumerable swarms of contractors – revenue officers, etc. etc. who in monarchies fatten on the miseries of the

43

poor. High and above all in influence and power, the clergy of the Established Church took a decided stand against innovation, many of them affecting to believe that dissenters were fomenting the dissatisfaction of the people, to promote the dissolution between Church and State! I say affected, for no sensible right-minded man could believe such monstrous calumnies, against this numerous respectable body, who could count amongst them a vast number of those most distinguished for piety, work and intellect.

The Reformers, like their opponents formed an heterogeneous mass. Some of the friends of this alleviating measure who anxiously feared for the political salvation of the country if some reform in manifold abuses did not take place, were first in talents, rank and wealth." [...] Gentleman who: "were all men of great wealth and responsible stations, and were distinguished for information and integrity. Many of the latter rank were our particular friends[...]"

"The Register firmly, but moderately espoused the popular cause, and was open to discussion for and against the great question, which then pervaded the public mind: it was the only paper in the West Riding (of York) which openly, and candidly, avowed its sentiments on political subjects."

In May 1791 Gales printed an unsigned article titled "The prospect of general enlargement of liberty opened by the revolution in France." This "enlargement of liberty" is not just a question of other European counties achieving liberation from despotic rule but is now explicitly linked with parliamentary reform and abolition of other abuses in Britain. These are now seen as facets of the same movement. Already in the previous year he had listed the 40 boroughs where the total parliamentary electorate was less than 40, including 9 where it was less than 10, culled from official papers which he described as "an authoritative statement of the inequality of parliament." And in his brief account of Edmund Burke's *Reflections on the French Revolution* he defends the principles of the London Revolution and Constitutional Societies as being reasonable and justified namely:

- all civil power derives from the people
- abuse of power justifies resistance
- the rights to private judgement, liberty of conscience, trial by jury and the freedom of the press should be inviolable.

In 1791 *The Sheffield Register* prints a succession of news items, articles and letters interspersed with occasional editorial comment extolling liberty and reform. Initially these are expressed in general terms or refer to events in other towns and cities as the Sheffield reform movement was not established in an organised form until the year end.

In March he prints the resolutions of the Manchester Constitutional Society founded in October 1790. In April there is a reprint of an article in *The Analytical Review* commenting on Thomas Paine's *The Rights of Man Part 1*, published the previous month which is described as "one of the most curious, original and interesting publications which the singular vicissitudes of modern politics have produced." Paine himself is described as "a stern republican who exults in Liberty and treats with equal freedom the monarch and peasant alike." There is a letter containing a florid soliloquy in praise of the French Revolution and liberty and in a later edition a poem celebrating the Revolution and criticising Burke. A news item describes an event in London where a 1000 "gentlemen at the Crown and Anchor" (the well-known Whig tavern) celebrated the 2nd anniversary of the Revolution in France. After the usual liberal toasts to the freedom of the press and trial by jury there were toasts to "Perfect freedom instead of toleration in matters of religion" and "To the literary characters who have vindicated the rights of man, and may genius be ever employed in the cause of freedom." Finally, thanks were offered to Mr Burke for the discussion he has provoked which was received with much applause. At this stage there was still widespread support of both the changes in France and reform in Britain. This would soon change.

In the summer of 1791 *The Sheffield Register* is already recording or engaging with the actions of the opposition which had begun to mobilise and take the offensive. One is the first of Gales' frequent attacks on what at this stage he calls the "ministerial prints" later more usually termed "the hireling press." In July he observes that these "prints, having exhausted their powers in casting obloquy on the revolution in France" have the effrontery to set their faces against Sunday schools. "The peasantry of the country [say they] will derive more advantage from the plough and the spade than from the horn book and primer." Behind this attack was the fear that if the lower classes learned to read they would be open to subversive influences and less willing to be subordinated to the control of their masters.

Also in July he reports on the riots in Birmingham and the burning of the houses of some prosperous dissenters including Joseph Priestley. The first of his reports on these riots seem to regard the disorder as the spontaneous actions of an unruly mob but in August he reports on an advertisement by Birmingham Dissenters offering a reward for evidence of authorship of forged letters intended to "delude the populace and instigate them to violence against dissenters." These attacks were to be repeated in many other towns across England over the next few year and future editions of the newspaper would contain further reports, letters and editorial comment on these subsequent events.

❧❧❧

They Burnt his Books and Scared his Rooks: 27th July 1791

In June 1791 and act of parliament permitting enclosure of large parts of Sheffield received royal assent.

The enclosure of common lands had been going on throughout England over the preceding century and was supported by many progressive people, including a correspondent to *The Sheffield Register* in 1787, as the only way of increasing food production to feed the growing urban industrial population. In practice, however, it resulted in rich landowners taking over the commons and excluding poorer people, who had previously been able to graze small numbers of domestic animals without charge and supplement their food or income.

The previous enclosure of Ecclesall which extended right up to Crookes Moor, took place in 1779. This enclosure had included land on which the Sheffield races had taken place and brought about their demise (the course running from the modern day Broomhill along Fulwood Road). That they were deprived of this popular entertainment no doubt still ran strong in people's memories and in the folklore.

This latest 1791 enclosure act was also set to take away many open spaces from around the town: in Heeley, Newfield, on Crookes Moor etc.

The implementation should have come as no surprise. For more than a year *The Register* had printed a succession of public notices and factual reports announcing the pending enclosures and the enabling act of parliament. This act authorised the total enclosure of a number of commons bordering the town and the dismantlement of all encroachments: vegetable plots and small workshops which had grown up over time.

The main landowning beneficiaries were to be the Duke of Norfolk, the principal landowner in the town, and the Vicar of Sheffield, the Rev. Wilkinson. (In a sense, it could be said that the philanthropy of a later Duke of Norfolk in creating a park for the citizens of the town, was little more than repairing some of the damage done by his predecessor.)

These enclosures provoked a reaction that earlier enclosures had not. The factors were presumably the wide extent of the act: affecting lots of inhabitants who were being deprived of access to a public amenity used for recreation: a feeling of entitlements being removed. This has to be coupled with the growing politicisation, resentment towards those in power, and doubtless, on the part of some, sheer bloody-mindedness.

It was the act of implementing the measures that started the chain of events. When the Enclosures Commissioners: Vicar Wilkinson and Vincent Eyre, the Duke of Norfolk's agent were attempting to mark out the enclosure boundaries they were driven off by a crowd of local people.

The civil authorities applied to the government for assistance and on 27th July a detachment of light dragoons arrived at the Tontine Inn from Nottingham. This was a very provocative act: strong-arm tactics from outsiders having echoes of Orgreave down the centuries.

This was the trigger for disorder: people responded by attacking, in turn, the prison (with a nod to the Bastille?), followed by Vicar Wilkinson's Broom Hall, and the residence of the Duke of Norfolk's agent. More soldiers were sent from York to restore order.

That Wilkinson was the target probably follows not just from the enclosure, but from building resentment against him following the execution of Stevens and Lastley and also for his sanctioning of the digging up of graves when Church Street was widened (He was the "black, diabolical fiend" of Mather's song *The Black Resurrection*. A popular song arose from enclosure riot: "They burnt his books, And scared his rooks, And set his stacks on fire—")

The Sheffield Register reports the events as follows:

> "The sudden news on Wednesday morning, of a party of soldiers being expected in town, excited alarm of some, and the curiosity of all. A great concourse of people went out to meet them and on their entering the town, the streets were lined with the populace. The people thus got together, did not, during the day wholly disperse; but, as evening drew on, the number increased, so that by nine o' clock many hundreds were in front of the Tontine Inn. Such an assemblage of persons, of various descriptions, not the most peaceably disposed, needed only a pretence to be mischievous. This pretence occurred, and the gaol was the object; the doors and windows of Mr Fox's house, [i.e. the gaol] were soon entirely demolished, and the prisoners of course liberated.
>
> The unthinking multitude, thus successful in their first outrage, pursued their violence. Broom Hall was now their cry – the house of the Rev. Mr Wilkinson our vicar. All the windows were broken, part of his furniture and library

damaged and burnt, and eight hay ricks set fire to, four of which were entirely consumed. Before the populace had been long at Broom Hall, they were followed by the Light Horse, who presently dispersed them. Thus disturbed, they returned to town, and broke the windows and did other damage to the house of Vincent Eyre, Esq. The dragoons were however presently at their heels, and drove them from their new object, and so successful dispersed them, that no farther mischief was effected.

The soldiers remained on guard all night, and in the morning two troops of heavy dragoons arrived form York. Several of the acting magistrates who had been sent for express, attended at the Tontine Inn, and swore in a great number of additional constables, who patrolled the streets the whole day. This step, with others equally spirited and prudent, and the great activity of the soldiery, put and end to an unhappy riot, for which we are at a loss wholly to account."

This report was preceded by this editorial observation: "On Wednesday, at noon, arrived here from Nottingham, a detachment of Light Dragoons, in consequence of an application to government for them. The grounds which gave occasion to this application were, we believe, a violent repulse given to the Commissioners of the Inclosure of Stannington and Hallam, in this neighbourhood, some days ago, on their attempting to mark the boundaries; as well as from several suspicious persons having come into the town from Birmingham, since the riots there, who had, it is said, made some attempts to stir up a spirit of dissention among certain inhabitants. Whether these circumstances were, or were not, of sufficient magnitude to authorise this measure we shall not take upon us to determine. Neither shall we make a single comment upon the following facts, but leave every one to draw his own conclusions." (This suggestion that *agents provocateurs* may have been involved is interesting. Was a justification needed to bring about a clampdown? What other motive could there be for men to come from Birmingham?)

In *The Register* of the 5th August, however, Gales is less hesitant and says: "Much praise is due to the Magistrates for the spirited vigilance, with which they embraced every means of checking the tumultuous proceedings of the populace. " He also says: "we are in no small degree indebted" to the "activity of the constables" and the "intrepidity of the military" for their role.

On August 19th he reports on the trial of the three of the five "deluded youths" (all under the age of 19) who were sent to York Assizes "heavily laden with irons" for their involvement in the riot. The government were "determined to spare no expense in bringing to punishment all those who should be guilty of the offence."

The prosecution was selective in its determination. The evidence against John Bennett was that he set fire to books and a table in the Rev Wilkinson's house and took a lighted candle to his haystacks in the yard. The others who he was with "absconded." Two youths, Benjamin Johnson and Thomas Furniss who had tried to demolish the gaol had the charges against them dropped, one just as the judge was about to sum up the case. This was said by the counsel for the Crown to be because they did not "wish to punish with a vengeance." Bennett was sentenced to be hanged.

Charges were also dropped against the other two, Ellis and Frogatt, by proclamation. The authorities had their condemned man to act as a warning to deter others "from future lawless and wanton acts." Bennett was perhaps a very easy scapegoat. According to the publisher and chronicler, R.E. Leader he was "a half-witted fellow who had been employed by the mob as the monkey used the cat to take chestnuts from the fire."

Gales moralises on the verdict as follows: "...we feel ourselves called upon most forcibly to beg the serious attention of those misguided persons who have been active or instrumental in the late riots, to the situation in which their misconduct has plunged them. From the fate of Bennett, thus cut off from the society his own folly had made him unworthy of, at so early an age, unthinking youths and wicked men may draw this salutary lesson: that the vengeance of the law is sure to overtake their crimes; that an ignominious fate must be the inevitable consequence of their attempts to injure the property of individuals, or of resistance to the laws of the country: that youth itself cannot save the guilty."

Gales initial reluctance to commit himself may have been no more than a prudent caution about commenting too quickly on very recent events for fear of distorting the truth or it may have reflected genuine misgivings about the decision to call in the military. His subsequent more forthright condemnation and declaration of support for the authorities may also be partly a product of politic self-interest rather than total conviction. But these reports also demonstrate his profound disapproval of mob violence and his abhorrence of civil disorder. These are attitudes and values consistently maintained and asserted over the next two years and need to be borne in mind when we evaluate later events and accusations made against him.

Liberty!

The new French Constitution and the rights it guaranteed was printed in full in *The Sheffield Register* in August and September 1791. Though not at this stage accompanied by editorial comment, the factual report highlights for readers some of the relative shortcomings of the current English system in terms of both liberty and representation, though many of its elements had been operative in England since the 1688 revolution. The Constitution guaranteed:

- That all citizens are admissible to places and employments without any distinction but that of ability and virtue;
- That all contributions [to state expenditure] shall be divided equally among all the citizens in proportion to their means;
- That the same crimes shall be subject to the same punishments, without distinction of persons;
- Freedom of movement and assembly, freedom of writing, speaking, printing and religious worship;
- Liberty to do whatever neither injures the rights of another nor the public safety;
- The inviolability of property or indemnity if the property be required for public purposes;

- A public fund for the relief of the infirm or unemployed
poor

The constitution set the rules of eligibility for voting for members
of the National Assembly with definitions of French nationality and
a minimum contribution to the national exchequer equivalent to
three days' labour. The proposed distribution of seats took account
of population. There was also a declaration that France would not
undertake wars with a view to making conquests and would not
employ forces against the liberty of any people.

At a later date in recognition of the interest generated by
publishing this constitution Gales reprints it complete on a large
sheet of paper for convenience of framing. This too must have been
experienced by his opponents and detractors as provocative.

The Sheffield Constitutional Society

The first meeting of the Sheffield Constitutional Society – a society
to bring together those wanting to campaign for reform of the
constitution – took place in the autumn of 1791. It has been
suggested that Joseph Gales was a founder member and that he
continued as a committee member but the evidence does not
suggest that he was a regular attender at its meetings over the first
two years or that he was active in its ongoing organisation. He did
however print its notices as well as some of its publications and
several letters generated by its establishment and progress.

In December one of Earl Fitzwilliam's intelligence gatherers in
the town wrote to him stating that "no person of consequence has
come forward to join the reformers except a Quaker Physician
named Sutcliffe." And in the following month another wrote to
Fitzwilliam stating that the "society was composed almost entirely
of the inferior sort of manufacturers and workmen."

The Constitutional Society printed its first notice in *The Sheffield
Register* in December in order to refute accusations "of some
designing people" that they were "dangerous mobs" whose aim was

to subvert the constitution, and to declare that their only aim was to achieve by "peaceable reform" a more equal representation of parliament, and to invite people to attend their meetings to see the "order and regularity" of their proceedings. An important aim of the Society was to "disseminate knowledge universally, more especially that species of knowledge which immediately concerns our fellow creatures and human beings."

In a second notice printed in February 1792 the Society announces a division into two meetings because of growing numbers, and 6d admission charge with tickets purchasable in advance, and requests "that no persons will attempt to intrude themselves into any of the above assemblies, merely from an idea of gratifying an idle curiosity or with a design to create confusion and disorder," this request being made "in consequence of the behaviour of a certain person who attended their last meeting."

By June the membership had grown to 2000 and they had been compelled to reorganise themselves into a series of small groups meeting at different venues, each group sending delegates to a central meeting. There were of course constitutional societies springing up around the country but Sheffield had possibly the largest membership outside London and the most preponderantly lower class membership. The explanations for this phenomenon partly lie in the high level of literacy and the employment patterns and religious affiliations of many of the townspeople. Furthermore, the existence of a newspaper like *The Sheffield Register* was probably a contributory factor, with its emphasis on truthful factual reporting, and the coverage it had given to the French Revolution and subsequent developments in France. One can deduce from the comments of correspondents that the newspaper reached a wider readership and audience than might be assumed by its circulation figures – though the circulation was high for a provincial paper – with joint subscriptions being taken out by the less well off and news items letters and articles in the paper read out and discussed in gatherings of neighbours.

The Society also published a range of pamphlets which were sold and distributed among members including a 6d edition of Paine's *Rights of Man* on 20th May 1792.

There were also a number of letters in *The Register* over these first few months, more or less supporting the Society. In late December 1791 a correspondent who signed himself 'Vicinus' (neighbour – now believed to be a friend of the Gales, John Payne) wrote that change would not come from the privileged, and criticised the inactivity of middle class groups who had previously espoused the cause of reform, adding that hopes are raised when we see "a love of letters and thirst for knowledge prevailing in the lower order of the community." In April another correspondent acknowledged that most of the members were journeymen, but supported their right to be heard provided that they eschew violence. A third correspondent who had attended a meeting of the Society expressed some misgivings at extreme views expressed by a few of those present while maintaining that these were not the preponderant opinions and urging that "a party of intelligent gentlemen" should regularly attend the meetings to effect a moderating influence.

In April there was one critical letter from a correspondent who had been to one meeting who found that "a spirit of sedition brooded among its members" and complained that it "was not governed by men of respectability and knowledge of our constitution and form of government." This prompted another correspondent to reply that when he attended a meeting he was impressed by "the spirit of order" which pervaded their meetings pointing out that at inception they had invited men of property to join them but none had done so.

The overall impression one gains from this correspondence was that occasional middle class attenders at the meetings of the Society formed contrasting views mainly because of differences in their preconceptions rather than because of their actual observations. Whatever the efforts of the Society to profess its peaceful intentions and allegiance to the Constitution many members of the propertied classes had profound misgivings about the very existence of an organisation whose aim was to raise the awareness and knowledge of working men with regard to political issues.

The Execution of Spence Broughton

Another trial where there was a whiff of blood money affecting the outcome was that of Spence Broughton, the last man to be gibbeted in Sheffield. Broughton was involved with two others in mail robberies. The robbery of the post from Sheffield to Rotherham took place in February 1791: the post boy's pony cart being stopped and the boy blindfolded and tied to a hedge. One of his accomplices escaped from prison in mysterious circumstances the other gave evidence against him and so escaped justice.

The Register in April 1792 carried a report of the trial "from a gentlemen who attended court." It is a detailed report and suggest that Gales had someone tasked with acting as a court reporter. He also has an interesting editorial comment on the value of deterrent sentencing, which still resonates today:

"Attercliff Common is reported to be the place where Broughton is to be hung in chains. Alas! 'tis pity such spectacles are thought to be necessary! Many an innocent mind will be greatly hurt by the horrid sight, and we fear the guilty are too callous to be affected by any sight – or how can we account fro the frequent robberies which are committed under the very gallows?"

For over twenty-five years the whitened bones of Broughton could be still be seen, with the rags of his clothes fluttering in the wind, on a post at the side of the road that now bears his name.

A New Clerk for the Register

In March 1792, there is an advert for a clerk. This post was filled by James Montgomery, a young Scot who was then residing in Wath on Dearne and working in a shop. Winifred describes him as "the amiable, the intellectual, the pious." The appreciation was mutual. Montgomery says of Gales: "… had all the reformers of that era been generous, upright and disinterested like the noble-minded proprietor of the Sheffield *Register;* the cause which they espoused would never have been disgraced. And might have prevailed…" Montgomery is better known by posterity as a hymn writer and poet, partly as a result of his own revision of his radical past.

Montgomery was provided lodgings at the premises in Hartshead. His contribution to the Register was significant, though it is not known the extent to which editorials were contributed by him.

Cutlers' Wages

On August 17th 1792 Gales prints a lengthy letter signed: "A Journeyman Cutler." The author who describes himself as "a poor mechanic, the inventor of arts and friend of genius" sets out in detail his annual income and expenditure with a view to demonstrate why though "sober and industrious" he cannot maintain his family – consisting of a wife and four children – because of the lowness of wages and high cost of provisions. His budget includes £4 per annum rent, £2.10s coal and water, £6.6s clothing, £1.10s soap and candles, 8s8d assessment for poor relief and highways maintenance, 6s window tax, and 18s for sick club payments. From what he says are typical cutler earnings of 12 shillings per week or £31.40s per year only £15.5s 4d remains for provisions which works out at 10d per day for the family or less than 2d per day for each family member. He points out that he also has to be responsible for the repair of his tools and he regrets that he cannot give his children any education. If he misses work through illness he has no choice but to go into debt as the sick club payments are insufficient to pay for provisions and fuel for a family of six. If his debts mount and he cannot manage repayment, he is confined to prison, half starved and prevented from working. If as a consequence his wife applies for parish relief she is only granted such relief if she agrees to the eldest child aged 7 being put into service where he experiences "every kind of hardship."

The only response, using the age-old argument that the poor

cause their own poverty, is a letter the following week signed "A Reader" arguing that a cutler's wages were much higher than stated though setting out no figures to support this. He states that the problem is that the workers will not exert themselves to work as many hours as their masters required and that wages were spent in idleness and debauchery. He acknowledges that there are many skilled workmen in the Manor gaol for debt – at a time when another correspondent is complaining of shortage of labour – and that most journeymen are in debt to their masters having received advances to purchase tools, but states that the fault is theirs owing to "that general depravity of manners which so greatly prevails amongst the working mechanics."

Gales prints these letters without editorial comment. Despite his concern for the poor he consistently avoids taking sides in any disputes between masters and workmen – see the report on the scissor manufacturers dispute in 1790. This may simply be that from commercial self-interest he may have been reluctant to risk alienating his customers and advertisers, but this is possibly too simplistic an explanation. As a printer Gales was an employer himself and it can be noted that all his references to the "alleviation of poverty emphasise philanthropy, moral reformation and keeping prices down not wage increases."

Gales was also a pragmatist, however, when it came to business. His was not a philosophy of "levelling," or seizing property or wealth. He published for example a letter explaining that:

> "The *Equality* insisted on by the friends of Reform, is an equality of rights, or in other words, that every person may be equally intitled to the protection and benefits of society; may equally have a voice in the election of those who make the laws by which he is affected in his liberty, his life, or his property; and may have a fair opportunity of exerting to advantage any talents he may possess."

Also, despite the Galeses stance against slavery ("the idea of purchasing slaves of trading in the blood and sinews of our fellow beings was most revolting to our feelings") they found on arrival at

Raleigh in North Carolina, where the labour market was slave dependent, that they could not operate their business without some reliance on slaves, at least in the early days. In Gales' own words: "from necessity, we were induced to purchase several, both as house servants and to aid us in the conduct of our printing, paper-making and farming concerns."

Constitutional Principles or Seditious Doctrines?

By 1792 the previously slumbering giant was sat bolt upright in bed – there were several factors at play.

There was a growing sense of disillusionment amongst reformers as they realised that the "general enlargement of liberties" envisaged in the heady days after the French revolution would not come about in England without making parliament more widely representative. On the restricted parliamentary electoral roll, control was firmly in the hands of the privileged and their nominees with the consequence that progressive legislation in the wider public interest was repeatedly blocked.

Improved communications and the ready access to printed material was also very empowering for reformers. Constitutional societies sprang up in other towns in addition to Sheffield and London, and they corresponded with each other – exchanging views and ideas for organising – all "breathing the principles of the Constitution as established in 1688," according to Winifred. She quotes the lawyer Erskine, who went on to defend Tom Paine and to represent many of the Jacobins put on trial for treason. This is from a speech delivered at the meeting of the "Friends of the Liberty of the Press" in December 1792, which she says was in the spirit of the times: "If in the legal and peaceable assertion of freedom, we shall be calumniated and persecuted, we must be content to suffer in its cause as our fathers before us suffered: but we will, like her fathers, persevere, until we prevail."

The second part of Paine's *Rights of Man* came out in February of

1792, containing a revolutionary ideas about redistribution through fair taxation and a system of social security, that it would take until the 20th century to start to be realised. The book was soon widely circulating in cheap editions, published by the constitutional committees.

Gales printed extracts from the First Part of the book in *The Register* starting in April 1791, and copies were soon on sale in the Galeses shop. Winifred says that, they sold hundreds of Paine's works and printed thousands by order of the Constitutional Society.

In Sheffield it was said that every cutler had a copy. In June 1792 Colonel Oliver de Lancey, the Secretary of War's Deputy Adjutant-General, carried out an assessment of the disposition of troops in Sheffield as part of a government mission to ascertain the state of the country and the measures needed to curb any unrest. The letter reporting his findings survives. In it he says that in Sheffield "the seditious doctrines of Paine and the factious people who are endeavouring to disturb the peace of the Country, had extended to a degree very much beyond my conception, and indeed they seem with great judgement to have chosen this [town] as the centre of all their seditious machinations." Paine gave the SSCI permission to publish a copy of the first part, which was sold at 3d each.

Sales were no doubt boosted by the Royal Proclamation issued on the 21st May 1792 against seditious publications, effectively banning The Rights of Man. (Would The Sex Pistols *God Save the Queen* have ever made number one in the UK charts without a ban?)

The Disturbances in Sheffield on May 11th 1792

In March 1792 *The Register* reports the arrival of two troops of dragoons to be quartered in the town. At that time there were no barracks in Sheffield and troops were quartered with the civilian population. Gales criticises the London papers for false reporting quoting them as saying that the arrival of the troops has put an end to the disturbances in the town whereas the truth was that the town had been quiet and peaceable since the troubles during July of 1791.

On May 11th there were further disturbances in Sheffield which Gales reports as follows:

> "It is an unpleasant task, to record circumstances which tend to lessen in any degree the credit which inhabitants of this town have obtained, of being generally inclined to peaceable and orderly conduct; and if we except the unhappy disturbances of July last, and the present uncomfortable state of things, we shall find the good opinion above formed, to be a just and decided one. We should be sorry to censure unjustly; and as opinions may differ, we do not presume to offer our own ideas as to the cause of this disturbance, we shall only say, it is generally attributed to disputes which have arisen in the streets, betwixt the officers of the troops now quartered here, and sundry of the inhabitants, who conceive themselves injured by the officers' conduct."

He continues by describing an assembly of people in support of the "offended party" in front of the Tontine Inn shouting complaints against the officers and the breaking of several windows. There was a further gathering two days later when the military "doubtless greatly irritated" rushed out and threatened the crowd and when they did not disperse pursued some of them to different parts of the town and maimed many innocent unoffending citizens. Gales praises the actions of some of the principal inhabitants and the magistrates who were brought in, the former being praised for their efforts to deter the military and the publishing of a conciliatory advertisement pledging to support any individual who has been unjustly treated. At the time of printing he reports that although the town was still in great confusion, "all was at peace."

On May 18th he reports that this "huge and populous town is again tranquil thanks to the people accepting the assurances of the principal inhabitants" and he further reports that "the officers who have been so largely blamed have now left town."

In his reports of the riot of the previous July, Gales held back from criticising the military and eventually praised them for their cooperation with the magistrates in restoring order. This time while avoiding direct criticism of the military the suggestion that they were the cause of the trouble is clearly implicit in his report and he is able to make this point while praising the magistrates and the towns leading citizens.

These events, combined with a recognition of the dangers of the whipping up of hysteria against the enemy within, was no doubt behind a notice which the Sheffield Constitutional Society inserted in *The Sheffield Register* on June 4th containing a declaration approved by the various fortnightly meetings of the members, though the notice states that they are responding to misrepresentation in various "daily prints said, and generally supposed to be under the immediate influence of the present administration."

This declaration denies any attempt to foment revolution or overturn the constitution and again affirms that their sole objective is a reform of parliament consisting of equal representation and annual elections. They further declare their abhorrence of all riots and disturbances. They condemn all "wicked and seditious" writings and say that they are happy to see persons writing or publishing such punished by due process of law, but they protest against the right of the Secretary of State or any other individual of whatever rank "to be allowed to make any publication be considered as wicked or seditious, because he is pleased to term it so." These decisions should be taken by a jury. This declaration and subsequent ones by the Society was published under their own logo containing the maxim "*vox populi – vox Dei.*" (The voice of the people is the voice of God.)

It has been suggested that Gales drafted some of the Society's resolutions and undoubtedly the style of some of this shows some sophistication not untypical of his writing but there were other members of the Society such as Enoch Trickett who could write well, as is instanced by his subsequent letters to the newspaper.

Time and time again their cause of seeking only equal representation was put. But the bandwagon of state propaganda was now rolling and picking up speed...

The Liberality and Tolerance of the Nobility

In May 1792 Gales had commented in *The Sheffield Register*: "There appears to be a general alarm in the minds of men on the progress of the spirit of reform in England. That the spirit of reform is awakened every man must see but there is nothing that can make it alarming save the fastidious pride which sets itself in opposition to the common sense and common good of man."

Nevertheless the alarm continued to grow, fuelled by the growth of popular movements and events in France. The privileged and propertied felt their interests threatened and in particular feared that an extension of the vote to people with little or no property would undermine their dominance. Antagonism and resentment built up towards those who were seen as encouraging the poor to assert themselves and abandon their customary subservience. Writers such as Paine and newspaper editors and booksellers who promoted the circulation of reformist and radical ideas among the people were often the focus for anger and resentment.

Although this was a national phenomenon, a town like Sheffield found itself at the centre of such antagonisms because of the sheer strength and numbers of its popular movement, and also because of the lower class base of most of this support. In Sheffield the pro-government forces found it impossible to mobilise a popular reaction which could cow or suppress the actions of the reformists. In the surrounding towns and villages the reaction was much stronger and more immediate. For example, in May, Gales reports "a noble earl, owner of a large property not more than a 100 miles from Sheffield" gave notice to quit to a tenant whose family has been tenants for near 100 years "avowedly for no other reason than that he was a professed admirer of the constitution of France and a friend of the Sheffield Constitutional Society." He adds that this is "a specimen of the liberality and tolerance of the nobility and hereditary legislators of Great Britain." If the said "noble earl" was Fitzwilliam, Yorkshire's Lord Lieutenant, whose residence was just twelve miles from Sheffield, Gales was already making dangerous and powerful local enemies.

The royal proclamation condemning the writing and publication of seditious writings prompted meetings throughout the country to pass resolutions thanking the King for his intervention and endorsing the royal sentiments with implied threats to the perpetrators. Several towns near Sheffield passed such resolutions and a public meeting was called in Sheffield for the same purpose on 11th June 1792.

This meeting was convened by a local worthy, Dr Brown, at the town hall which then stood on a corner near the parish church, on Church Street. There was a large gathering, and one of the Sheffield Constitutional Society men, William Camage, spoke against the motions to "thank his gracious majesty for his attention to the welfare of his subjects in prohibiting Paine's writings." His argument was, according to Winifred, that such measures were not called for and were aimed more at causing division and bad feeling toward the friends of reform and therefore they couldn't allow such a sentiment to go forward in the name of the citizens of Sheffield. There followed a "violent philippic" from the Revered Russell, "who disgraced the cassock which he unworthily wore." The motion was overwhelmingly rejected.

The "Church and King party" then called a private meeting two nights later in the Cutlers' Hall, which they advertised by a handbill. Those attending this second meeting were confronted by a crowd of opponents who, though denied entry, held their own meeting in the street outside.

Gales prints an account of the events which followed in a Register editorial where he defended himself from accusations that he had led and encouraged the mob.

Winifred also gives an account of the evening. Gales was having tea at home with Lord Effingham's land agent when alarming shouts called their attention to a growing situation where the crowd outside the Cutler's Hall were threatening to tear it down. Winifred describes how her husband and his guest "ran immediately without their hats." When he arrived the Revered Mr Radford, vicar of Trinity Church, was "haranguing the crowd." Though Joseph said: "a respectable and worthy character was thus addressing them: 'Why will you be thus violent, gentlemen? Are we not all Englishmen?

And have we not one common interest?' " Gales was called by acclamation of the crowd to take the chair and he was carried "bareheaded to the seat which Mr Radford had rapidly vacated."

The best account of what happened is given by Winifred:

> "A few plain sentences appeared best to suit the occasion, and in his usual quiet and composed way, he enquired 'if the large assemblage of people he saw were there in consequence of the handbill that day issued.' A few voices answered: 'Yes.' 'Did you intend to sign the vote of thanks?' Several voices moderately answered: 'No.' 'Then my friends you have certainly no business here. You expressed your sentiments yesterday, and you would surely not deprive your neighbours of the same privilege. Hitherto Sheffield has been celebrated for the orderly and peaceful conduct of the manufacturing part of the community. Do not now forfeit your claims to this honourable distinctions.' Several voices said, 'Speak on Mr Gales, You are a good man, we will mind what you say.' 'If you rely upon my advice,' answered your father, 'because you believe me to be your friend, I will prove it to you, by recommending that every man opposed to the object of the meeting depart peaceably home. Oblige even those who differ in opinion with you, to respect you, by shewing that you respect yourselves.' 'Home – Home' was the general cry, and in twenty minutes not one of the opposition thousands there assembled, were to be seen."

Gales concluded his editorial with the following words:

> "I have no motive but honest principle, no reward but public favour, and no party but that of the truth. I pledge my credit as an honest man, that no threats shall deter, nor any temptation allure me, to depart from the rule of right, which I conceive to be essentially necessary for the real welfare of my country. The liberty of the press is essential to freedom, and the purity of its source is a public blessing, in no instance am I conscious of having violated it; and when the *Sheffield*

Register ceases to be a friend of virtue, however depressed and held down by poverty, when it is no longer the open and avowed enemy to vice, though gilded with all the pageantry of titles and wealth; and when it ceases to be a friend of the people, may it cease to exist."

Another account of these events is contained in the Joseph Mather song *Britons Awake*. According to the compiler of his songs, John Wilson, the crowd accompanied Gales back to his home singing Mather's *God Save Great Thomas Paine*.

This was not the end of it. Winifred continues that there were:

"men illiberal enough to be angry that your Father had so easily settled what appeared, and really was really a tumultuous and disorderly assembly. 'See' said an anti-reformer, 'what influences Gales has over the multitude if he speaks, their wild ravings are hushed into gentle murmurs. By what means has he obtained this dangerous influence?' One of his own political party answered: 'By pleading the poor man's cause, by advocating equal representation; by treating them as brethren. Gales is a good man, a friend to the oppressed, and a most exemplary man in all his domestic relations.' This spoke a person, who though opposed to Mr Gales, was too upright himself to withhold justice from another. 'Yes! Yes! We all know that, but so much the worse – there's the rub, for so much greater is his influence. He could lead 10,000 men by the crook of his finger, and if French principles should take root what would be the effect of his popularity?'"

The address to the king that was sent had on it less than a hundred signatures.

The Influence of *The Register*

For most of 1792 *The Sheffield Register*, in promoting this cause, did so not chiefly by means of direct editorial comment but by inclusion of letters and quotations from, and summaries, of pro-reform articles. True to the letter, if not the spirit of the promise in his founding editorial, Gales also printed letters from opponents of reform but these were incisively challenged by pro-reform respondents and the balance of the argument was always in favour of the latter. There is a question over to what extent this correspondence was all spontaneous or whether some letters were prompted, or even commissioned from the editor's friends, such as those of Joseph Payne as "Vicinus," or of James Montgomery.

There were a number of principal themes:

Firstly, there was information about the inequality of representation in parliament itself. Gales had printed a factual note on this in 1791 and the same issue was pointedly made by his correspondent "Vicinus" in January 1792 stating that the whole parliamentary electorate for England numbered less than one third of the population of Sheffield alone.

Secondly there was a differentiation of attitude and philosophy between the proponents of reform and the opposition such as was articulately stated in a letter printed in the newspaper on 28th September 1792. This letter includes quotations from the pamphlet written by the Bolton Unitarian, Thomas Cooper – *Reply to Mr Burke's Invective against Mr Cooper and Mr Watt*:

"…those who mean well to the people say, think for yourselves, read for yourselves, decide for yourselves; try all things, and hold fast that which is good: you are the most concerned in what relates to your own interest, and wherever you place implicit confidence, sooner or later you will be infallibly deceived. The other side on the contrary, take this for their text, and preach this for their doctrine: 'You (the people) have nothing to do with politics; leave it to your rulers, they know best what is good for you; you have no need to think for yourselves, pay your taxes quietly, and they

will take care to think for you."
Thirdly was a catalogue of the abuses which they believed could only be removed by a parliament truly representative of the people and not just privileged sectional interest. These abuses included discrimination against dissenters, compulsory church tithes, the game laws, navy recruitment via the press gang and the high level of taxes without public accountability as to how the money raised would be spent.

On the question of taxes there is an amusing letter from a correspondent from Gotham, south of Nottingham, who signs himself "Tom Ploughshare" questioning where his taxes are spent. He says that: "Though I am only a country farmer, and work hard for my living, yet I can manage as to spare a bit of money to join my next neighbour at taking in your newspaper." He claims to be often sorely puzzled at words he finds in the newspaper for "want of knowing learning, and new fashioned words." He had never been more horridly puzzled than when his wife and lasses "would need have me to read them the news of the fine dresses" at the Queen's Ball. "We were sorely afraid that our rents and taxes would be raised to pay for this vast finery." He adds with mock concern the unwanted influence on the fashion aspirations of his daughters and wife of these reports, but they could not "find out what in the name of fortune some of these things the women had on were made of." They conclude that *turban* must "most likely mean turnip; so I tell our women, it happens is the fashion to wear turnips, and would have them go to our church with a turnip on their heads, and two or three feathers out of our white cock's tail stuck into them, for fashion's sake." Similarly they conclude that *coquelicot* is something, to do with chocolate and *crape lamé* something to do with lime-wash – "happen London folks called "lime" *lame*, when they speak fine."

Gales himself in an editorial comments on the huge levels of expenditure on state functions and finery pointing to the expenditure of £1 million on a coronet, £100,000 on court dress and thousands on a feast at a time when poor people were imprisoned for small debts though his explicit primary concern is the need to legislate against imprisonment for debt rather than the curtailment of such extravagance.

Recruiting parties were generally reviled – for taking bread-winners away, and for tempting apprentices to abscond from their indentures. One such report on the recruiting parties talks of "the ear-piercing fife, and spirit-stirring drum. Recruiting parties flow in from all quarters, and very high bounties are offered. The street are paraded with colours flying, and – to suit the taste of Sheffielders who are well known to love good eating and drinking – they carry with them roast beef and strong beer, temptations too powerful to be resisted [...] they eagerly enlist, and fancy themselves lads of mettle who are desirous to serve their country, by giving the Spanish a hearty drubbing." There are also opinions stated that the need for press gangs to snatch and compel men to crew the warships would be removed by a substantial increase in wages but suggests that these are not approved by parliament because its members would not agree to measures whereby "the overgrown fortunes of rich landowners derived from monopolies of wastes and commons would experience an almost imperceptible diminution of wealth." (The full name of the Sheffield enclosure act was "An Act for dividing and enclosing several Commons and Waste Grounds, Common Fields, and Mesne Enclosures, within the Manor of Sheffield, in the West Riding of the County of York,)

In February 1792 Vicinus challenges a previous correspondent, J.T. (John Taylor, who will appear again in this story as the editor of the *Courant*) who had written that "in the present state of present affairs, we had every reason in the world to be contented and happy," contrasting it with what he believed to be the miseries of other countries. Vicinus replies accusing the previous correspondent of citing highly questionable hearsay information about life in foreign countries and continues:

> "I will contrast this with what happened in my own [country].
> Mary Jones was executed a few years ago. I well remember
> the circumstances. It was one of these occasions when
> pressing was resorted to; her husband was carried off by a
> press gang, her goods seized for some debts of his, and she,
> with two small children, turned into the streets a begging; she
> was under 19 and went into a linen draper's shop, took some

68

coarse linen off the counter, and slipped it under her cloak; the shopman saw her, and she laid it down: for this she was hanged. Her defence was (the trial is producible) 'That she lived in credit, and wasted for nothing, till a press gang came and stole her husband from her, but since then she had no bed to lie on, nothing to give her children to eat, and they were almost naked, and perhaps she might have done something wrong, for she hardly knew what she did.' The parish officers testified to the truth of her story at her trial. When she was brought to receive sentence she behaved in such a frantic manner as proved her mind to be in a distracted or desponding state and the child was sucking at her breast when she set out for Tyburn!"

Vicinus continues by urging J.T. to stop regaling the public with assertions that the people of this country are, a laborious, protected and happy people, "happy in all conditions," and asks if he is aware that press gangs have been lately resorted to again "on pretensions trivial indeed."

At times the debates between the friends and opponents of reform in the correspondence became so rancorous that Gales used his editorial position to urge moderation of language and abstention from personal animosity, in one case even declaring that he had "softened the language" in some instances prior to publication.

In the last editorial of the year, Gales comes out into the open stating that he has decided to clarify his political stance in view of the risks of misrepresentation. He affirms that he is a supporter of the British Constitution of 1688 of King, Lords and Commons (thus openly repudiating republicanism) but "cannot admire and revere the defects and abuses which Time and corrupt men have introduced into the system – the principal of which is the notorious unequal representation of the people in parliament (and which if repaired would, it is generally believed, remedy every other grievance)." He states his belief that any man can serve his country best by doing all within his power to produce conviction in the minds of the people with regards to this fact and adds: "This conviction must be brought about by the wise and temperate efforts of moderate men." He continues: "To the proprietor of this paper this middle path appears the wisest, which lies between the well intended but perhaps too great ardour of the Friends of Reform on the one hand – and the abject timidity of those who cherish prejudices, however contemptible, merely because they are prejudices, on the other."

Where you view the middle path as sitting depends on where you consider either extreme in the debate to be. It is not possible on the evidence, however, to regard Gales as the dangerous revolutionary that the establishment later tried to depict him as being.

Portrait of Joseph Gales. Courtesy of the State Archives of North Carolina. (If anyone knows the whereabouts of this portrait, or whether a possible portrait of Winifred Gales survives, please do get in touch.)

Sheffield as seen from Attercliffe Rd in the 18th century

Britannia from the *Register*'s masthead, astride Sheffield manufactures:
"silver plated goods" and "cutlery wares"

Part of an advert for rat poison

The device at the start of editorials

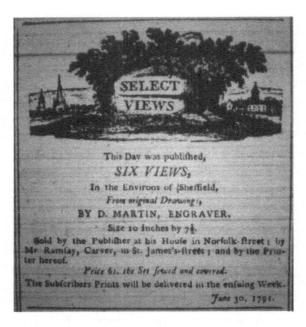

This Day was published,

SIX VIEWS,

In the Environs of Sheffield,

From original Drawings,

BY D. MARTIN, ENGRAVER.

Size 10 inches by 7½.

Sold by the Publisher at his House in Norfolk-street ; by Mr Ramsay, Carver, in St. James's-street ; and by the Printer hereof.

Price 6s. the Set sewed and covered.

The Subscribers Prints will be delivered in the ensuing Week.

June 30, 1791.

Advert for Martin's engravings

The halfpenny duty stamp found on each copy

The *Register/Iris* office in Hartshead

The Old Cutler's Hall 1638-1832

Henry Yorke

The grave of Joseph Gales (courtesy of Raleigh City Cemeteries
Preservation Inc)

The Parish Church of St Peters (now Sheffield Cathedral)

The Peasants are Revolting

Sheffield now increasingly found itself targeted by the pro-government supporters in a centre of unrest and potential rebellion.

Colonel de Lancey's letter of 13th June 1792, drumming up support for internal repression, contains the following – you can almost hear him foaming at the mouth – at Sheffield he found that: "seditious doctrines of Paine and the factious people who are endeavouring to disturb the peace of the country had extended to a degree very much beyond my conception." He reported that: "as the wages given to the journeymen are very high, it is pretty generally the practice for them to work for three days, in which they can earn sufficient to enable them to drink and riot for the rest of the week. Consequently no place can be more fit for seditious purposes." Two thousand five hundred "of the lowest mechanics" were enrolled in the principal reform association (the Constitutional Society): "Here they read the most violent publications, and comment on them, as well as on their correspondence not only with the dependent societies in the towns and villages in the vicinity, but with those in other parts of the kingdom…" and that their language "is the most violent and indecent that can be imagined." He also harshly criticised the effectiveness of the civil power in the city including the magistrates who he asserted "scarcely deserved the name." As an example of the lack of "opposition given by the magistrates and others to the unreasonable demands of the populace" he cites the case of the Duke of Norfolk's colliers who refused to work unless their wages were raised. The magistrates refused to get involved and the miners got their way. These disputes he said "must very materially hurt the trade of the place by enabling other countries to undersell them."

He was also concerned that the soldiers billeted in the town were turning native. They were "unavoidably exposed to hear their seditious doctrines in all the publick (sic) houses in which they are billeted […] and at this time when men's minds are in such a ferment then there is no saying how rapidly and how far it might extend." He wanted them in barracks out of town "free from the dangers of corruption."

De Lancey's report was deliberate propaganda aimed at convincing the Government of the need to erect permanent barracks in the town to enable strong military intervention; more for the purposes of social control than security. It cannot be read as an impartial or honest assessment; it seems clear that what limited evidence he gathered he took from a narrow stratum of Sheffield society. The declared aims of the Constitutional Society and the reports of outsiders who attended the meetings – with one exception – do not corroborate his observations, and almost any edition of *The Register* will provide evidence that the magistrates were diligent and far from lenient.

However, the barracks were built, and very quickly: construction started on barracks for 200 cavalry for the purposes of internal repression in July 1792 at a site off the present day Infirmary Road and was complete by 1794 (Barrack Lane is named after this – the new barracks at Hillsborough followed in the 1800s). Public money was readily found that was not available for either the Infirmary or a new workhouse, and no doubt reports like De Lancey's were influential in shaping the perception of the town among the government and their allies.

❧

Songs and Roast Mutton: Autumn 1792

The monarchies of mainland Europe viewed the events in France with horror and led by the Hapsburg monarch, Leopold II and the Prussian monarch, Frederick William II formed an alliance to stop the spread of revolution. France was forced into war to defend the revolution as troops massed on her borders. A Prussian army led by The Duke of Brunswick assembled on the Rhine and they issued a proclamation intent on restoring full powers to the French king. Brunswick's army invaded France in August following the storming of the Tuileries Palace.

Their march to Paris was checked at Valmy on 20th September, and the Prussian army drew back. The French monarchy was formally abolished the following day and the First Republic declared.

When the news filtered through to Sheffield it prompted open celebrations on the streets. On 15th October *The Register* reports that the news was celebrated in Sheffield with bonfires and firing of guns. Sheep were roasted and songs were sung. A pole was erected near to one of the fires on which the Cap of Liberty was fixed, and which bore an inscription written by "a journeyman grinder":

> "As citizens of the world, we rejoice that twenty-five millions of our brethren have nobly dared to break the bonds of slavery, under which they have for centuries groaned. We also rejoice that they are so intrepidly driving the armed despots out of their Republic. We sincerely wish, that their hostile brethren, the Austrians and the Prussians may learn from the French, the blessings of Liberty, and in their turn drive the tyrants from their land; and that Universal Freedom may take place of that Slavery under which Europe has so long groaned."

Elsewhere, an American flag was hoisted with the motto "May tyrants cease, and liberty flourish." The editor comments that the French victories had: "chased despondency, and inspired a hope that twenty five millions of people will transmit to their descendants, the blessings of Liberty and Peace." He adds that "the evening passed in a most orderly and peaceable manner, much to the credit of the people assembled, who generally were of the order of society (working mechanics) who, when invigorated by the joy-inspiring bowl, sometimes forget themselves."

In correspondence the Sheffield Constitutional Society comments on these events: "If any of our friends chose to rejoice at the success of the French armies, what harm did they do? They compelled no one to rejoice with them contrary to their own sentiments and paid for their own mutton and ale."

The newspaper reports further celebrations on 27th November following the success of the French armies in 'liberating' Brussels. An ox was purchased, suspended between two trees and roasted all night. The next day it was quartered and drawn through the streets amid firing of cannon and the cheering of five or six thousand people, three quarters being distributed to the poor in different parts of the town and the fourth quarter to the prisoners in the gaol. In the procession was a caricature painting of Britannia with Burke riding on a swine (Burke's characterisation of the English lower classes as "the swinish multitude" was deeply resented and provoked many such responses) and a caricature of "the Scotch Secretary" attempting to drive Britannia back into a pit with a spear while the Angel of Peace puts forward one hand to raise up Britannia and the other hand holds out a copy of Paine's *Rights of Man*. Two white banners were fixed on long poles crowned with caps of liberty with inscriptions. On one was written: "The French, by their arms, have conquered Tyrants; and by just Laws, Liberty and Reason will conquer the world" and on the other: "The glorious conquest of Brussels in which Life, Liberty and Property were secured even to the vanquished." Subsequently the crowds who had cheered the procession went into the Parish Church and rang the bells.

❧

Just Because You're Paranoid...

From early 1792 rumours were circulating that Christopher Wyvill who had led an earlier campaign for parliamentary reform was considering re-starting his campaign. These rumours were reported by a correspondent/spy of Earl Fitzwilliam, Henry Zouch, in letters written to the Earl (held in Sheffield Archives).

Make no mistake, the British aristocracy at the time were not some set of bumbling benign fools, as popular culture has often caricatured them to be. This was a deeply political set of people with a stranglehold over power, calculating, and ruthless. This is Winifred's "pro aris et focis" – a fight for everything they held dear: for hearth and home/ for God and country – keep what is ours by divine right.

In May 1792 the Sheffield Constitutional Society was contacted by the M.P. Charles Grey, a known supporter of political reform who had recently formed the Society of the Friends of the People. Fitzwilliam complained to Zouch that Grey's involvement would provide "the Leaders they had been looking for." This was no doubt viewed as a very dangerous development by the ruling classes. Here was a growing popular movement allying itself to serious politicians – presenting the possibility of unstoppable momentum towards reform. They had to find a way to split the two. What better way than to criminalise the popular movement and to spread hysteria of an enemy within.

Were the rumours of "suspicious persons having come into the town from Birmingham, evidence of an orchestrated stirring up of trouble designed to bring about repression?

In the autumn, with some sense of frustration, Gales observes that the only argument put forward by the opponents of reform was "to plead for the extension of the strong arm of power for suppressing discussion of all subjects relating to government."

They did not have long to wait for the repression. In December, in the national news section of the newspaper, the king –presumably on the instigation of, or with the full collusion of the government – recalled parliament on the grounds that the "spirit of tumult and disorder" in the country renders it necessary that strong action is taken "in support of the chief magistrate" (i.e. the king himself). To achieve this end it was judged necessary to "mobilise part of the militia of the kingdom." Later in the month legal proceedings were instituted for prosecuting Tom Paine, in his absence, for sedition. This was not just a theatrical gesture but was considered a necessary precursor to prosecuting printers and booksellers in order to suppress his works.

The local news section of the paper gives accounts of the actual mobilisation of parts of the Yorkshire militia and of more sinister developments – the provoking of the mob to attack and intimidate the supporters of reform. There were two such incidents reported in December, a mob attack in Birmingham instigated by circulated handbills where a house was attacked and damaged by a group of men who called themselves "the loyal true blues." The family were forced to come to the window and repeat the slogan "Church and

King" and 6 guineas were extorted from the householder before they agreed to depart. Later in the month there was an attack in Manchester on the premises of the printer of the pro-reformist newspaper *The Manchester Herald* and on the house of its proprietor Thomas Walker. Again there were shouts of "Church and King" and damage done to both properties. The mob did not disperse until three in the morning.

There is no direct proof that these and subsequent similar riots were directly instigated by government agencies or whether the similarities were a result of enthusiastic pro-government supporters copying one another. E.P. Thompson discusses the evidence for outside manipulation of the mob by the establishment encouraging the spread of false information and exaggerating the threat of disorder and rebellion in order to divide and weaken the pro-reform opposition and alienate its more moderate supporters.

The passing of a series of resolutions at public meetings in major towns throughout the country and the similarity of their wording certainly suggests an orchestrated approach. Resolutions were printed in *The Sheffield Register* from York, Wakefield, Chesterfield and Nottingham all declaring that they would endeavour to do all in their power to suppress seditious publications which disturb the peace and bring to justice their authors, printers and publishers, and especially such persons involved societies and combinations for the dispersion of such principles.

On 31st December a meeting was convened in Sheffield in the Cutlers' Hall, chaired by the Rev. Wilkinson, to pass such a resolution but although this was a private meeting with restricted entry – previous events having demonstrated the impossibility of getting such a resolution approved at an open access public meeting in the town – the wording was different from that passed in other towns. The Sheffield resolution acknowledged that it was a time of national alarm but expressed confidence in the continuation of tranquillity in the town. The signatories to the resolution resolved to use all their powers to maintain this and to give strong support to the civil government and magistrates to suppress all riots and violent and tumultuous disturbances.

The Sheffield resolution contained no reference to prosecution of authors, printers and publishers, nor to societies promoting such views and its tone and omissions enabled Gales to comment in the newspaper. "A declaration was read which from the very moderate and liberal manner in which it was written was adopted without any dissenting voice and we doubt not of its receiving very generally the signatories of the inhabitants."

The recognition by the government and its supporters that in Sheffield the reformist cause had very widespread support among the people resulted in it being targeted in the campaign of false information calculated to promote and incite public alarm both within the neighbourhood and elsewhere. Both Gales and the Constitutional Society were constantly having to use *The Sheffield Register* for refuting such false information. One such false report, in what Gales contemptuously terms "the hireling press," was that a Sheffield mob stopped Earl Fitzwilliam's carriage and removed two of the four horses saying two were enough for anyone. Gales states that everyone in Sheffield knows this to be a lie. Later the Constitutional Society condemns as an "unproved falsehood," a "calumny" by a Birmingham clergyman that the Society have so far adopted levelling principles that they had measured the land around Sheffield for distribution.

The accusation that the reformers were "levellers," that they planned a wholesale redistribution of property and wealth from the rich to the poor, was the one which the government and its allies realised was most likely to be effective in weakening support for the reformist cause. Gales was driven to print the following refutation in his 14th December editorial. He points out that even in France, "where a most total revolution has taken place," ownership of property has been safeguarded except for property belonging to the church, crown and émigré enemies of the state. He adds that such accusations are "an insult to common sense and humanity" and contrary to the fundamental interests of fathers, husbands and tradesmen, in that the security and wellbeing of their families would be threatened by implementation of such principles.

The events of December undoubtedly threw the supporters of reform on to the defensive. In many parts of the country support for reform was weakened and in towns and cities such as Sheffield and London, where the movement held its ground, its supporters were more isolated and therefore more easily targeted.

❧

A Working Man's Perspective

On 31st December *The Register* printed an open letter to members of the Constitutional Society. The writer who signs himself "A Reformer" urges the members of the Society, his fellow townsmen, to continue to testify by their behaviour that the true spirit of liberty is the spirit of order and by this means refute and defeat the "numerous calumnies, of those who from mistaking your views, or other motives, misrepresent your real designs."

This letter prompts an interesting reply from a working man who signs himself: "A Manufacturer:"

"As it is Christmas time, I invited a few neighbours to sit with me one evening and to smoke their pipes, and we belonging to the Constitutional Society, began to talk about the news, and one of them took up *The Sheffield Register,* and read us a letter signed a *Reformer*. Now we all thought it a fine piece, and hoped our Society would mind what it said, and follow all the good advice it gave us about being orderly and quiet, and so I hope we shall, for as to riots and tumults we abominate them. But says one of the company, you are all very sensible we have many great lies told of us, and fulfil the old proverb 'Some folk had better steal a horse than others look over a gate;' for if there be any riots, I'll lay all I am worth to a three-penny pair of scissors, that the other side raises them – though you may be sure we shall bear the blame, even though we could prove we had been fast asleep at the time. Now I'll give you an instance. Take any of the resolutions different towns have passed (for except ours of Sheffield they are all partly copied from one another) and you will find that they are set out against Levellers, and against seditious writings and tumults. But I'll put a case. Suppose we and some more of our friends were to go into any of the next towns, to a public house, and say we were come to hold a Constitutional Society, and try to get a more equal Parliament, let us behave ever so civilly, we should soon have the constables, or parson, or the Lord knows who, to turn us out, and talk of putting the landlord down for harbouring us. Now let us go there again the next night, drest like blackguards, and carry a bundle of straw or old rags with us for an image, and say it is Tom Paine we are coming to burn, I'll lay, the constables will say nothing to us, or happen some gentlemen of the town will join us on horseback, give us money to spend, so we may get drunk, fight and swear Church and King as long as we please; and if any man offers to hinder us, ten to one they'll whisper that man is a republican, and then we break him a few windows, as the Church and King fellows did at Manchester."

After further observations on seditious writings, Tom Paine, levellers and the way middle class supporters of reform have "turned tail" he concludes: "We all thought our neighbour said right, so after drinking, Peace to the world – Liberty of the Press – A free Parliament – and, The Reformer's health, may we all practise what he advises – we parted in good time.

"Sir, if you please to put this in your paper, you may alter it if you have a mind, if I have put the words wrong, and you will oblige a constant reader."

Gales adds the following footnote: "We have not availed ourselves of the liberty the correspondent has given us of 'changing his words,' any further than in a few places in the article of spelling; because we judged that most of our readers would be better pleased to see the home-spun effusions of a plain man, just as they come to us, than when corrected according to rule. If however he chuses to write again, we wish he would submit his letter to the correction of some ingenious friend, before it is sent."

Prosecution of Booksellers and Printers

In the first half of 1793 *The Sheffield Register* reports several instances of booksellers and printers being prosecuted for distributing allegedly seditious material – principally Paine's *The Rights of Man*. These included the Newark printer, Holt, Phillips, the printer of *The Leicester Herald*, and booksellers: Bower of Winster and Thompson from Birmingham. Bower was acquitted by a Derby jury, as had been the secretary of the Derby Constitutional Society, previously prosecuted. Gales commends the Derby jury for their liberality and their love of liberty and justice by "dismissing vexatious suits instituted to restrain the freedom of the press – the great palladium of British freedom." Thompson was also acquitted by jury but not before spending several months in prison awaiting trial, with his correspondence and access to friends and family severely restricted by the keeper of the gaol.

Winifred Gales writes about Holt who she describes as a young man of respectability and talents who partly learned his business by working with her husband: "Poor Holt was found guilty of publishing a treasonable pamphlet, and was sentenced to 4 years imprisonment and to pay a fine of 200s. He outlived his sentence, but his constitution was injured, his prospects in life destroyed, and he did not long survive his liberation, leaving a destitute family." Phillips received an eighteen-month sentence and a heavy fine. She also mentions William Birch who along with a man called Falkner published a popular paper in Manchester. They were indicted, but fled the country, Birch later becoming one of their friends in America.

She also rails against the injustice that you could be prosecuted for having sold *The Rights of Man* before such a time as it was declared libellous (*ex post facto* law). She writes: "Was it not painful to live in a country, when the expression of honest opinions, in a man's professional vocation laid him open to tyrannical prosecutions and when he might unwittingly and unconscious of evil commit offences against a law, passed six months after."

In the case of Phillips, Gales alleges in *The Register* that the jury was hand-picked by the Deputy Bailiff, father of the Town Clerk who brought the charges, and that Phillips was denied the right to challenge the jury.

These events prompted interesting correspondence. Our

previously quoted correspondent who writes under the name "A Manufacturer" again takes up his pen to gave expression to his deeply felt concerns about injustice and unfairness:

> "Sir, I wanted to tell you how me and all my neighbours are grieved and surprised to see it in the news concerning the taking up a shopkeeper and a poor working man in Birmingham, and chaining them down like thieves, only for selling and reading a book. If it be true, what a sad pass things are come to in England! Ruin a tradesman, and chain a poor working man down to a bare board in a prison, like the poor blacks (God help and free them I say) on shipboard, and all this for reading Tom Paine, as they call him. Why, Sir, it's talked on in almost every shop in Sheffield, and all round the country, and they say it is a barbarous thing, and what Englishmen will soon grow tired of – for if every man that has read Tom Paine was to be handcuffed and chained down to a bare board in a prison there would not be folks enough left to chain and fasten their next neighbours. And if our great folks would not have the book read, why did they not stop it at first, and not let it go till everybody had read it, and then punish them for it. – And then they say again, it was not done so to those scoundrel dogs who robbed and burned so many houses and chapels – no, they got winked at, and laughed at it themselves. So it looks as if some folks thought that reading Tom Paine was a worse deed than burning a house."

Referring to Gales previous request about drafting of his letter he says he has talked to a young man "that's clerk to a friend of mine about it, and he said he had heard one say, they could not spell words and letters wrong when they printed." With typical Sheffield 'cussedness,' he adds that consequently he has not complied with the editor's request saying: "Sir, if you please to set out this letter, I am sure you can do it right, without my getting a friend to do it, and if it be a bit of trouble what signifies that, why I am a customer of yours." This was too much for Gales who was so overworked at the time that he shortly announced his decision to scale down his auctioneering business to give more time to his newspaper. He comments that he has inserted the letter "to oblige our customer" and because the sentiments of every class of society on interesting topics merit attention, but says that the trouble of correcting the spelling and punctuation is so considerable that he will decline further correspondence from the writer unless he complies with the editor's original request.

In a very different letter in March 1793, another correspondent argues that changes in and current interpretations of the libel laws are a dangerous infringement of English liberties and a major erosion of press freedom. "Since some late transactions, I have been inclined to think, that a libel is not any real and positive thing; but that men of power and profound learning can make a libel just how and when they please, of anything or nothing, and I should not wonder if it soon becomes a prevailing fashion to call everything a libel that honestly exposes the faults, and clashes with the pecuniary interests of great men [...] Should the nation be hurried into an unnecessary, pernicious, and destructive war, will it be a libel, to say it ought not to have been so?" With reference to Burke's characterisation of the English populace as the swinish multitude, he asks: "Is it a libel for the *swinish multitude* to grunt?"

No charges or proceedings were brought against Gales or any other Sheffield printer or bookseller at this stage – not until the middle of 1794 when the repression was intensified. This may have been partly due to Gales shrewdness in his choice of words and his anticipation and avoidance of the risks. But it would seem likely also that the local civil power and in particular the resident magistrate the Rev. James Wilkinson made a deliberate choice to avoid or delay moving against him. Gales had supported Wilkinson consistently on both public order and philanthropic causes, but the canny Wilkinson's main reason was probably that his priority was the maintenance of public order in the town and a recognition that this could be put at risk if any such proceedings were instituted. This could also be the reason why the meeting chaired by Wilkinson on 31st December 1792 adopted a much less confrontational wording in their resolution than that passed by other towns.

Confirmation of the caution of the authorities is given by

Winifred Gales for the lack of persecution at this time, despite the paper and sales being more prominent in the public eye than those of others prosecuted. "We lived in Sheffield, in the hearts of the people, who would have risen en masse at any intemperate proceedings – two-thirds of the people would not inform – the rest dare not. And theses feelings were proved for we had sold hundreds of Paine's works [...] and had printed thousands by order of the Constitutional Society!"

Intimidation of Reformer and Dissenters

Elsewhere in England the process of intimidation continued through 1793 with parades and ritual burning of effigies of Tom Paine who a *Sheffield Register* editorial says "was butchered in every petty village in the kingdom" as well as by "the pious rabble of Birmingham" and some other large towns. He continues in the same vein of heavy irony:

> "Paine has suffered universal martyrdom. At parish and corporation meetings he has been condemned by bell, book and candle, and punished with fire and faggot! – all which he has supported with the philosophic patience of an archbishop! In short, no primitive martyr could have borne a tithe of the hanging and burning he has done! – In one parish he was burnt for being a Presbyterian – in another for being a Jacobite – in a third for being a *Popish Jesuit* – and in a fourth for being no less than the *Devil himself*! – Though we do not altogether subscribe to so black a charge as the latter, yet we cannot help thinking that he must be something more than a man, who, at the close of the eighteenth century, can work such wonders simply by the magic incantation of – *a goose quill?*"

Sometimes these activities took an uglier turn, demanding a more serious tone in his commentary. He describes how the house of a

Manchester cobbler was attacked and all its windows broken because he was thought to have cut down a dummy serving as an effigy of Tom Paine the mob had previously "executed" by hanging. More serious still is the account of events in Macclesfield where an "outrageous mob paraded through the streets" carrying an effigy of Tom Paine, "made of a long pole, and an old coat and hat hung upon it." This mob made a "sudden and terrible attack against the house of Mr John Bacon, ironmonger, and broke open the shop door, with a heavy volley of stones." Both Bacon and his son were grazed by flying stones and they tried to seize the son when he tried to pacify them. The threat was made that they would "pull down the house and kill them." After firing shot over the mob had no effect, John Bacon fired small shot into the crowd slightly injuring several people. Gales concludes his report: "Mr Bacon and his son are now lodged in jail, and no bail will be taken. – As friends to peace, and feeling, as we do, for the laws and liberty of subjects of this realm, we sincerely sympathise with the unfortunate sufferers in the above very alarming infraction on both."

There are also reports in *The Register* of mob attacks on property in Nottingham, Bristol and again in Birmingham. In the latter it is stated that a dissenter chapel was destroyed.

These actions had their effect but not always what the government intended. In June 1793 Gales writes: "We are sorry to learn from various quarters, that a number of respectable families, chiefly among the Dissenters, have it in contemplation to remove to America, under the idea that their persons and property are now exposed to the insults of bigots and mobs. [...] America will doubtless receive the voyagers with open arms and will be glad that so many virtuous men, and ingenious manufacturers, are come among them; but we can ill spare such – our country requires the united aid and support of every wife, liberal and candid man."

Two months later Gales reported that the emigration to America has increased to such a degree that according to the London press the government was intending to introduce laws to prevent such emigration: "It does not look well in a Government to force its subjects to be contented at home!"

There is very little record of attacks of dissenter or reformist households in Sheffield, nor is there any record of the burning or hanging of effigies of Tom Paine in the city. The reason for this appears to be that the level of popular support for the reformist cause in Sheffield was so much higher than support for the Church and King party.

Poetry of Protest

Around this time *The Sheffield Register* starts printing some verse of genuine quality in its poetry column: poems which articulate the frustration and dignified resistance of the people to the injustices they suffer. The Armytage paper in the *North Carolina Historical Review* suggest some of these have been attributed to the pen of the "editor's brother Timothy Gales who came to assist him at this time." But this is problematic, and it is not clear where Armytage gets his suggestion from. Joseph Gales' only brother Thomas died in 1787. There was a Timothy Gales, Joseph's grandfather, but there is touchingly understated report in January 1793 of the death in Eckington of Timothy Gales, "a respectable old man aged 83 years.")

Other poems were published anonymously but stylistic similarities prompt the suspicion that they may be from the same pen.

One such example is the poem which is terminated: 'Norton, April 8   T.G.' entitled – "No libel to think":

In a state of oppression, we'll *sigh* our complaints;
It may seal our destruction, to *tell out* our wants;
Tho' to speak we're forbid, our hearts shall not sink,
For we've freedom enough, while we've freedom to think.

We may speak (it is true) if we mind what we say;
But to *speak all we think*, will not suit in our day;
Tho' our tongues be cut out, or chained fast with this link,
Who dares say we're not free, while we've freedom to think?

They tell us our state is both perfect and pure,
The ills we point out, do not want any cure;
To believe such a doctrine, our reasons must sink;
So we'll think as we please, while we've freedom to think.

Can a man clothe his back, or eat his own bread?
Can he marry a wife, or bury his dead?
All such matters as these, will make his coin chink–
We can think of such things while we've freedom to think.

Can a man use his eyes, his hands or his tongue,
But must pay for the service these members have done?
And yet more than all these are just on the brink;
What strange thoughts we have while we've freedom to think!

From the sole of the foot, to the crown of the head,
They stamp us, and tax us, both living and dead!
And yet at such hardship they wish us to wink;
But we cannot do this – while we've freedom to think.

When the sunshine of LIBERTY breaks on our sight,
The reform of *Abuses* we'll claim as our RIGHT:
"The Friends of Reform" is the toast we will drink,
And we'll think of our RIGHTS – *while we've freedom to* THINK!

There is another well-written poem, possibly from the same pen:
"The Observations of a Swine" printed on 28th June in response to a
poem printed a few weeks earlier called "Patriotism." It goes to the
heart of the debate over whether common people had rights or
should just stay in their place. It opens:

Did Nature 'mean us to be slaves?'
The property of fools and knaves?
Have we no claim or just pretense
To common rights and common sense?
Or, will you have say the Hand divine
Made some for Lords—the rest for Swine?

On the same theme, but also possibly by the same person is a poem printed in July bearing the title "The Swinish multitude to Edmund Burke."

Be pleased, great Sir, to find us work
We make no insolent pretensions
To feast on sinecures and pensions;
We know our food must be the getting
Of our own labour pains and sweating;
Twas so, they say, in ages past,
And must be so while time shall last.
But, sir, though this is fit and meet,
We cannot quite forget to eat,
Nor miss our usual grains and water,
Without just asking, What's the matter?
You told us so, and we hop'd it true,
With folks above we'd nought to do.
We've nought to do, 'tis mighty plain,
With any thing our betters *gain;*
But when, they meet with checks and crosses,
We find a partnership of *losses,*
And must be *sconc'd* in work and wages,
Because crusading all the rage is.
    Now this we think not quite the thing,
    So pleased to hint it to the—

War with France

In January 1793 a *Register* editorial noted that war: "like an impending dreaded storm threatened misery to the country" and observed that the trade of Sheffield had already received a setback with orders cancelled in anticipation that shipping to the continent would be disrupted. War was declared in February and before the end of the month the newspaper was reporting the presence of thirty recruiting parties in the town.

Throughout the year the newspaper kept up a vigorous and unflagging anti-war stance by means of editorial comment, extracts from celebrated writers and barrage of correspondence.

In February Gales says: "the hundreds, nay thousands of human beings, subjects in a neighbouring nation are to be offered up, to expiate the loss of an individual, such is the world's mad business." He goes on to quote from a powerful piece written by the late Samuel Johnson on the miseries of war:

"It is wonderful with what coolness and indifference the greater part of mankind see war commenced. Those that hear of it at a distance, or read of it in books, but have never presented its evil in their minds, consider it as little more than a splendid game, a proclamation, an army, a battle, a triumph."

In March, an editorial notes the bloodshed and loss of life in a recent battle between the French and the Austrians and hopes that war can be ended without the same happening to British troops. He appeals to the government to listen to the voice of the people – the war was widely unpopular at this stage – and takes note of the sharp increase in business failures and unemployment.

But the Government and King were on a very different tack. During the same month the King called a general fast on April 19th urging that this be observed by "all our loyal subjects" and threatening punishment to all who do not comply. In the first edition after the fast, *The Register* reports that though "it was in general well observed throughout the country; in London (the very seat of authority) we learn that taverns were full and the churches empty; and that Mr Pitt himself gave a dinner to his friends!!"

Gales takes a swipe at the Church and King party, and their fast day drinking binge, adding that in Sheffield which is "stigmatized with being the seat of ignorance and disloyalty; an opportunity offering to rescue it from at least one part of the imputation, we embrace it, by giving the following liberal toasts; which were drunk, we are informed (if not true we shall readily contradict it) by a numerous and respectable company at the Bear in Norfolk St, a few days ago. – We previously however, beg indulgence for the authors of them, and hope our readers will not impute these sentiments to a depravity of heart, but to some other less blameable cause:

"May Tom Paine live for ever; may he never die; nor nobody never kill him; but may he be put in a bag, and hang swig swag over Hell's Gate, till doomsday!!!" And:
"May the Devil sweep Hell with the enemies of the King, and afterwards burn his brooms!!."

In a June editorial Gales quotes an unnamed writer who says that former wars always had a specific objective, however flimsy. War was initiated to weaken another nation because it was too strong, or to destroy it because it was too weak, to create a barrier, or because they were unwilling to adopt proposed treaties or because they adopted treaties one did not like etc. "But in the present war we are perfect strangers to the object it is to attain."

In October *The Register* reprints part of a poem by the Bishop of London, Dr Porteus. Porteus was a fierce opponent of the principles of the French Revolution and of Paine's work. So, this poem, written in 1759 in a different context, is being used to hoist him by his own petard (with upper case letters thrown in for extra emphasis):

'...ONE murder makes a villain,
MILLIONS a hero. Princes are privileged
To kill, and numbers sanctify the crime.
Ah! why will Kings forget that they are men?
And men that they are Brethren? Why delight
In HUMAN SACRIFICE? Why burst the ties
Of Nature, that should knot their souls together
In one soft bond of amity and love.
They yet still breathe destruction, still go on
Inhumanly ingenious, to find out
New pains for life, new terrors for the grave,
Artificers of death! Still Monarchs dream
Of Universal Empire , growing up
From Universal Ruin! Blast the design,
Great God of Hosts, nor let they creatures fall,
Unpitied Victims at Ambition's shrine!

The following month a correspondent who calls himself "An Old Whig" points to the failure to learn from the recent American War of Independence and suggests that even if the allied armies are successful in battle the French will be continually revolting against their conquerors and the consequence will be endless civil war. Another correspondent suggests that the only point to the war is to satisfy "the bloodthirsty ambition of those despotic monsters with whom we are combined" and a third accuses the Government of "not resting satisfied with continually quarrelling with our European neighbours and on every trifling occasion spilling the blood of thousands and ten thousands and entailing on our posterity millions of debt we have carried our desolation to distant lands" such as India.

The opposition to the war continued through into 1794 with a January editorial praising the Duke of Norfolk for his persistence in opposing the continuation of the war together with "a few other distinguished patriots in both houses."

‏‏‎‎‏‏‎ ‎‏‏‎ ‎‏‏‎ ‎‏‏‎ ‎‏‏‎ ‎‏‏‎ ‎‏‏‎ ‎‏‏‎ ‎✄✄✄

The Effect of the War on Britain's Poor

Throughout 1793 editorials and letters in the newspaper had made the link between the damage done by the war to business and trade, and increasing poverty due to unemployment and the lowering of wages for those who remained in employment, stating that all large manufacturing towns were seriously affected. In a May 1793 editorial Gates appeals for a fund to be set up to "afford poor, unemployed families a small pittance sufficient to save them from falling victims of famine and despair." The following story is printed in support of his plea:

> "Some days ago, one of those industrious mechanics at
> Manchester (of which we are informed there are at this time
> ten thousand) who are experiencing all the distress imaginable
> for want of employment, applied to the overseer of the town
> for relief. He was told that no relief could be afforded him.

'You are able (said the parish officer), to serve as a soldier: go
fight for your King and Country.' 'But (replied the suffering
artisan) I have a wife and four children, what will become of
them?' 'Go you for a soldier (rejoined the officer) and we will
provide for them.' The poor man almost broken hearted,
knowing his family to be in a famishing state, as the only
remedy left him, enlisted for a soldier. Mark the sad effect! He
hastened home to give his pining family food; but on
informing his wife how he had obtained it, 'that he was a
soldier, and that she and the children must go to the
workhouse,' the poor woman sickened, and in a paroxysm of
grief and despair, went out and hung herself!!"

The newspaper also reports demonstrations by hungry unemployed
workers in Manchester carrying the slogan "give us peace and
preserve us from starving." In one such demonstration, disturbance
broke out and eight people were arrested by the militia.

In another edition there is an account of an attempt by a group
of "villains" to break into a flour warehouse in Sheffield to which
the following comment is appended:

"It is much to be feared if the war continue, that the strong
hand of necessity will press on the lower classes of the
community, but let them consider that poverty is infinitely
preferable to disgrace and that they had far better await a
more prosperous trade than rush into crimes and ignominy by
continuing depredations on their neighbours' property.
Distress never yet appealed in vain to the inhabitants of
Sheffield and we trust that the affluent will never see their
brethren wanting the necessities which support nature but
they will with their wonted humanity contribute to alleviate
their distress."

Another editorial comment printed during the same month has a
different emphasis:

"He who has never hungered may argue finely on the

subjection of his appetite and he who was never distressed may harangue as beautifully on the power of principle. But poverty like grief has an incurable deafness which never hears, the oration loses its edge and 'to be or not to be' becomes the only question. There is a striking difference between dishonesty arising from want of food and want of principle. The first is worthy of compassion, the other of punishment."

There appears to be a difference in underpinning values and perhaps an implicit contradiction between these two passages. This prompts the question as to whether Joseph Gales was the sole writer of editorials at this stage of the newspaper's history.

৵৩৯৬

A Death and a Birth

In April 1793 there is an obituary:

"On Friday last, died suddenly, *The Sheffield Advertiser.* Having never been of a very strong constitution, it had evidently declined for some years past, and was not, in the common course of events, expected to survive long; it is, however, generally reported, that some sudden shock hastened its dissolution! Nay, some have not scrupled to say – and that with grave faces too – that this literary Phoenix was bribed to make away with itself! Be that as it may, it was quietly interned in the burial ground of Oblivion; where it sleeps so sound, that we are persuaded the last Trumpet itself will not break its repose – for its spirit was not Immortal."

Gales did not have a monopoly for long. This was perhaps what he was alluding to when he talked of bribery. Two months later, there appeared in the town a fierce and aggressive Church and King rag: *The Sheffield Courant,* printed by John Northall and edited by John Taylor. It was a different beast altogether: it never had a large readership but that was never its point. It was in effect a campaign mouthpiece, presumably bankrolled by supporters of Pitt's government, at some level or other, against the *Register* and the reformers with the objective of stirring up as much trouble for them as possible and bringing about the clampdown that Sheffield had not yet seen. To that extent it was successful.

The Sheffield Petition for Parliamentary Reform

In March a *Register* editorial comments: " from every part of the country we receive intelligence that the minds of the people are firmly determined to use every legal and constitutional exertion to obtain a moderate reform, and that no opposition whatever shall render them blind to their rights…" There were also reports of petitions from Scotland and Nottingham and the wording of those petitions printed.

It was in this context that a petition was prepared for Sheffield. On the 1st April Gales chaired a meeting of reformers at the Bull and Mouth pub in the Wicker to discuss "a proper mode of petitioning the House of Commons on the subject of a Parliamentary reform." This meeting arranged for a public meeting to be held on the April 8th to consider the petition, which was advertised in *The Register*.

As permission to use the Town Hall for the meeting had been refused it was initially called for the Bull And Mouth, but was immediately adjourned to an open air venue, Castle Hill, because of the large numbers wanting to be present. *The Register* states that several thousand people were present. Gales was voted into the chair of the meeting and the style and wording of the petition suggests that he played a major part in drafting it:

"To the Honourable the Commons of Great Britain in
Parliament assembled,
THE PETITION
of the inhabitants of the town and neighbourhood of
Sheffield sheweth,
"That the House of Commons is not, in the just sense of the

words, what the petitioners are from form obliged to term it, viz 'the Commons of Great Britain in Parliament Assembled' not being freely elected by a majority of the whole people, but by a very small portion thereof; and that from the very partial manner in which the members are sent to Parliament, and their long continuance there, they are not the real, and fair and independent representatives of the whole people of Great Britain.

Your petitioners are lovers of peace, liberty and justice. They are in general tradesmen, and artificers, unpossessed of freehold land; and consequently have no voice in chusing Members to sit in Parliament – but though they may not be freeholders, they are men, and do not think themselves fairly used in being excluded the rights of citizens. Their ALL is at stake, equally with the freeholders; and whether that all be much or little, whilst they pay their full share of taxes, and are peaceable and loyal members of society, they see no reason why they should not be consulted with respect to the common interest of their country. They think men are objects of representation, and not the land of the freeholders or the houses of a borough-monger.

It is not merely because heavy and grievous taxes oppress them, that your petitioners pray for a reform of abuses which are too notorious to be denied by the most prejudiced. It is as much in account of the application of that money, as of the money itself, for which they are concerned. They love their country, and would contribute a portion of their last shilling to support it, were they sure that every shilling was well expended. They pray for the correction of this abuse, because they are convinced that upon it depends the peace, happiness, and prosperity of their country.

That your petitioners wish the House of Commons to become the true representative, or judgement of the Commons of Great Britain, and the undoubted guardian of the interests of the people. That the delegates and their constituents may feel one common interest, Members of Parliament should be chosen for short terms; and descending from their delegated station, mix again with the people by whom they were chosen.

That the voice of the great body of the people ought not to be smothered by the voice of a partial interest, but should be fairly and fully heard: as nothing short of this will do away with that unhappy spirit of discontent which so generally prevails in our country; and this done, neither proclamations nor prosecutions will be necessary to secure tranquillity and peace.

Your petitioners therefore, relying with the greatest confidence on the virtue of some, and on the candour, good sense, prudence, and justice of all, hope this honourable House will take these premises into their serious consideration, and adopt such a plan of effectual reform in the representation of the Commons in Parliament, and of the duration of the same, as to their wisdom shall seem proper.'

The petition was unanimously approved by those present and parchment copies were placed in the shops of Gales and another bookseller for signature. 10,000 signatures were obtained, though local opponents disputed the legitimacy of this number on the grounds that women as well as men had been allowed to sign! Petitions carrying thousands of signatures from all round the country went before parliament at this time: from Norwich, Huddersfield, Derby, Nottingham, London, and 14 from different parts of Scotland.

The Sheffield petition was presented, in a somewhat lukewarm fashion, to the House of Commons on 6th May 1793 by Thomas Duncombe, Yorkshire's other MP besides Wilberforce. *The Register* reported on the proceedings. The government in the person of Dudley Ryder opposed the petition even being debated on the grounds that: "it was not worded in a manner sufficiently respectful to that House, and that they could not consistently with their own dignity receive it." (This view was shared by Wilberforce who called it "highly indecent and disrespectful.") Charles Earl Grey, however, reasoned that on the contrary "nothing could be so derogatory to its dignity [that of the House], as to encourage the people to state fairly their grievance, and then to turn short round upon them, and refuse to receive their petitions, upon a little inaccuracy of expression." *The Register* reported that Charles James Fox spoke in support of the petition being heard, arguing that "the best way to preserve the respect of the House was to shew a kindness to the people, and not to spurn them with disdain. William Lambton added, helpfully, that given that "the petition had been said to have come from ignorant tradesmen, and if so, polished language was hardly to be expected." Parliament refused to consider the petition, the vote count being 108 votes to 29.

How many blunt speaking Yorkshire folk have since had their views ignored for not wording them in the "correct" manner?

❧❧❧

The Most Useful Soldier in the War, Graffiti, and Buggering the King

With the government's refusal to consider the Sheffield petition and other such representations it was evident that reform of parliament would not be achieved in the short term. Although there was no change in values or in principles this resulted in a change in emphasis in the newspaper. There is a partial explanation of the bolder stance contained in an editorial of 30th May 1793. In this he recommits the *Register* to:

> "continue to be the Advocate of Misery, the Friend of Virtue, the Detector of Villainy, the animated Defender of Liberty – it shall still expose absurdity, ridicule Folly, resist Oppression…" He says he: "sees unconcernedly the feeble efforts of a proud Aristocracy, to check the powerful voice of truth and impartiality. The reasoning powers of men are awake, and they can see and judge between the subtle delusions of sophistry, and the convincing force of reason; they will behold with contempt the poor exertions which are made to subjugate their minds to oppression, and to fetter

free opinion (that inalienable birthright of mankind) in the despicable bonds of ignorance and superstition.
'There is no mind so ignorant, but the spider Prejudice can find room to enter it;' and therefore, the Editor is not surprized that his patriotic sentiments have created him enemies amongst those who think it compatible with Christian charity to endeavour to starve a man into political orthodoxy. Such is the conduct of a few individuals (whose poverty of spirit will punish itself) who boast that they have done and will do what they can to injure the Editor for daring to advocate the cause of freedom and the people. Their endeavours are like the exclamation of the fly on the chariot wheel, and the editor leaves them to the full enjoyment of the dust they fancy they have raised!"

Campaigning against the war comes to the front of the agenda as do the issues of freedom of the press and freedom of speech, by then under serious threat.

Gales also adopts a long-term perspective and appears to take his stance from Godwin's *Political Justice* which is quoted several times in editorials. Gales' objective is presumably to rally the spirits of the reform party by urging patience and persistence and assuring them that in the long-term success is inevitable. Three such quotes from Godwin are set out below:

"The legitimate instrument of political reformation is truth. Let truth be incessantly studied, illustrated and propagated, and the effect is inevitable. Let us not vainly endeavour, by laws and regulations, to anticipate the future dictates of the general mind; but calmly wait till the harvest of opinion is ripe. Let no new practice in politics be introduced, and no old one anxiously suspended, till called for by the public voice. The talk, which for the present should wholly occupy the friend of man, is inquiry, instruction, discussion. The time may come when this task shall be of another sort— Error being completely detected, may sink unnoticed into oblivion, without one partizan to interrupt her fall. This would inevitably be the event, were it not for the restlessness and inconsiderate impetuosity of mankind."

"Does any man assert a falsehood? Nothing farther can be desired than that it should be confronted with the truth. [...] Where argument, therefore erroneous statement, and misrepresentation alone are employed, it is by argument alone that they must be encountered. We should not be creatures of a rational and intellectual nature, if the victory of truth over error were not ultimately certain."

"In the invention of printing is contained the embryo which in its maturity and vigour is destined to annihilate the slavery of the human race. [...] Knowledge cannot be extirpated. Its progress is silent, but infallible; and he is the most useful soldier in this war, who accumulates in an imperishable form the greatest mass of truth."

Gales contributes directly to the debate by drawing on his knowledge of historical antecedents. He points to the meeting called in 1703 called to censure and forbid the reading of the celebrated *Essay Concerning Human Understanding* by the widely acclaimed philosopher John Locke and comments that at an earlier date the reading of the English Bible was similarly proscribed. Elsewhere he draws parallels between a recent trial of a man named Eaton for speaking allegedly seditious remarks in the street with the trial of William Penn in the reign of Charles II, noting that the jury returned verdicts of "not guilty" in both instances.

He laments the fact the "men of high talents" so frequently forget "the benevolent spirit which ever accompanies the truth." He continues: "To suppose that men are vile and dishonest and enemies to good because their opinions are erroneous, or rather because their opinions differ from our own, is one of the evils which deserves every exertion of genius for its extirpation."

The vast majority of the citizens of Sheffield did demonstrate a high level of discipline and restraint, and it is significant that unlike many other towns Sheffield had experienced no major disturbances since the formation of the Constitutional Society. (It is of passing interest to note that this temperament has continued to the present day. Sheffield experienced none of the rioting that others towns did in the 1980s, or early 90s despite being hit harder than most by government industrial policy. In the summer of 2011 it was the only large town in the country that the Tottenham riots did not spread to.)

For some, however, frustrations did boil over. It would hardly be expected that all of the ordinary Sheffield working people would find it easy to follow Godwin's advice about patience and study given both the frustration of their political aspirations and their sense of injustice and unfairness, at a time when many were suffering from extreme poverty through unemployment or underemployment.

Where deviations from the Society's commitment (their declaration of "utter abhorrence of all riots and disturbances") to maintain public order did occur it was in the actions of individuals or spontaneous non-violent demonstrations. The crime reports record a number of individual lapses. In one, a joiner, Francis Rodgers, was convicted by the magistrates for speaking treasonable and disrespectful words against the King and for being drunk when he uttered them. He was fined nine shillings.

In another incident a cutler and two gardeners from Sheffield were bound over to appear at Pontefract sessions for the same offence when sober. The latter incident prompts Gales to comment:

"As they are the first, we hope these will be the last instances we will have occasion to mention a want of respect for our Supreme Executive Magistrate, in any inhabitant of this town. If abuses have, from the lapse of time and the machinations of designing men, made their way into our Government (as no doubt they have) it is not any wanton, illegal expression that can remedy them. The only tendencies they have is to irritate the enemies of reform, and are means of throwing odium upon the best intentions of men, who earnestly wish for reform of parliamentary representation. All such expressions written on walls (of which we are sorry to say there are too many in this town) have the same tendency. We should be glad, therefore, to have both totally abandoned, as producing many bad effects, without any good one."

❧

The Crookesmoor Massacre and the Siege of Rotherham

However, when rumours of armed insurrection were circulating and there were reports of men performing military exercises on Crooks Moor he decides to adopt a different tone. In the paper on the 12th July 1793 he uses satire and ridicule in an attempt to counter what he sees as an over reaction:

"Brave Sheffielders! Surely this is an age where people strain at gnats and swallow camels! The simple circumstance of a few hearty fellows of the town, armed with broomsticks, and other equally formidable weapons meeting on Crooksmoor to learn the military exercise, with the murderous intent of killing time, has so alarmed the neighbourhood that no one can sleep in their beds for it. No sooner does the foxhunter lie down in his kennel, than he sees a Sheffield cutler pop through the through the window, and clap a huge mortar like a pocket pistol to his breast! When the squire closes his eyes, fancy transports him to Crooksmoor, and places him diametrically opposite a battery of ten thousand two and forty pounders, which discharging all at once in his face, blow out his brains – he stares – and finds himself in bed! The parson dreams of churches and steeples cutting capers in the air! The farmer sees his hay stacks on fire, and his harvest reaped with swords! In a word, at the name of Sheffield every face turns as white and grave as a judges wig."

This is followed by what Gales refers to as the Siege of R—! You can imagine the hilarity as this account was read out in the inns and taverns round town as they poked fun at the neighbouring town:

"Twas at the very witching time of night, and no longer since than last week, a cavalier, in common English a man on horseback, happening to canter pretty briskly up Westgate, the watchful sentinels awoke and gave the alarm! The drums beat to arms – every soldier yawned, rubbed his eyes with one hand and grasped his musket with the other – every man of spirit jumped out of bed, and with no other coat of mail but his shirt, no other arms but a poker, shovel, or mop, stood as big as Hercules at his own door; whilst the women and children screamed and huddled the bed cloaths about them – the dogs barked – the cats mewed – and terrible to relate the clock struck!! The report ran that all Sheffield was on its march, laying waste to the country with fire and sword! Whilst the enemy were invisible, heroism was visible, and triumphed in every countenance; but, no sooner did a quick-eyed wag swear that he saw our Old Church steeple, with the tri-coloured flag upon the spire, followed by all the roofs and chimnies of Sheffield, pass the Toll-bar, than every door was locked in a trice, and every soul sweating in bed, expecting every moment to be crushed in the ruins of their houses! – When the sun rose in the morning, he found Sheffield and Rotherham upon the same ground, where he left them the preceding evening, and both fast asleep."

Gales response to these events had two aims; to urge his fellow radicals among the working people to avoid provocative behaviour and to dampen down the alarm which was growing among the more prosperous classes in the town and neighbourhood. It would appear that he had more success in the first of these aims than the second.

The History of A Church and A Warming Pan

This was the title of one of James Montgomery's satirical pieces which was serialised by Gales in *The Sheffield Register* in August 1793, perhaps in accordance with Godwin's maxim that 'truth' should be illustrated as well as studied.

Montgomery writes an allegorical humorous fable of events in a village where over the years the parish church had fallen into disrepair by neglect and depredations by the village elite. The villagers were not overly concerned until two events heightened their awareness of pending disaster: a dream by the sexton's wife that the church had collapsed burying her husband under the rubble, and this dream reinforced by a farmer who swore that as he was returning from market one evening he met the sprit of the old church roaming the moor, as departing souls do before leaving their bodies.

All the villagers came to a meeting at the church where the parish clerk and parson regaled them on the urgency of the repairs and announced a monthly collection to assemble a repair fund. The mode of this collection was for the sexton to carry a warming pan round the congregation prodding each person until they put in a coin. The collections were raised from monthly to fortnightly, weekly and finally twice weekly and an association consisting of the squire, the parson, the clerk and their hangers-on was set up and met at the Crown and Anchor with the ostensible purpose of planning and commissioning the repairs. The collected monies were spent on rum and brandy by the squire the parson and their associates. Time passed without any repairs being initiated and then to the surprise of the congregation the clerk announced that the costs of collection and association meetings had been such that the fund was £50 in debt. Increased contributions were urged. Most of the congregation were gloomily fumbling in their pockets and were prepared to pay until a certain Tom Crabtree, staymaker, kicked the warming pan out of the hands of the sexton and denounced the squire, the parson and their associates. Crabtree said he had read in a book that all people were as equal as a box of dice or a shilling is to twelve pence and proposed that the Squire had his hair shaved and his teeth drawn out and the parson is tarred and feathered and the church blown up with gunpowder. The offending parties are then locked in the vestry.

At this stage in the proceedings a mysterious person whose name the author 'dare not mention' [whose words sound more like those of Joseph Gales than Tom Paine] enters the church and mounts the alter quietening the crowd by his natural authority. He urges restraint, avoidance of violence and respect to property and suggests instead that the guilty parties are forced to return the money they have plundered by lowering rents and forgoing tithes. The Church must be repaired unless a new one is built and for this purpose he proposes that the villages elect their own committee by equal representation of all the villagers. He then disappears.

Crabtree jumps up to urge his original proposal but his vigorous movement causes the vestry door to come off its hinges and pin him to the ground on which the villagers notice that the offending parties previously locked in the vestry have escaped through the vestry window.

❧❧

Debate Takes a Nasty Turn – Furious Party Spirit

In September a well wishing correspondent wrote to *The Register* warning the editor of the risks he was running, and urging greater caution and restraint. It was printed in full:

"I cordially join with your correspondent Pax, in his just eulogium on the moral tendency of the 'Sheffield Register,' and its uniform attachment to the cause of civil and religious liberty. At the same time, I cannot help lamenting, that a few intemperate, or unguarded expressions on political topics, have occasionally appeared in it; for though I firmly believe that such expressions ought to be attributed to an accidental oversight, or to the hurry in which a newspaper is always printed, rather than to design, yet they can do no good, and may possibly disgust some of your readers. Besides, a good cause disdains the aid of such expedients; it leaves invective of every kind, along with fines and persecution, to its opponents, and contents itself with a calm, manly appeal to the good sense of the public, and to the eternal principles of Truth, Reason and Justice. Nor should it be forgotten, that the times are now critical; that a furious party spirit now prevails, and seems to dispose some persons to watch for every inadvertent, unguarded expression; to give it a perverse meaning and then to expose the speaker, or writer, to the punishment of the law – regardless of the circumstances which might be adduced to lessen the offence, or the ruin which such severity may bring down upon a helpless, innocent family."

In reality, *The Sheffield Register* is surprisingly free of invective given the strong adherence to the causes it supports but some of the content was at times undoubtedly provocative to established interests however moderate the language. Following this warning, for the next few months Gales appears to have exercised greater caution in his editorial comments. But it was too late; enemies had been made.

In October 1793, the "furious party spirit" manifested itself in the first of a series of personal attacks on Gales published in the rival newspaper the *Sheffield Courant* mostly written by an Anglican clergyman the Reverend John Russell of Dronfield (a black hell-hound in Mather's song *Britons Awake*). His attack on Gales is vituperative:

> "in your seditious Register, you endeavoured to persuade the people that they were enslaved and wretched, although every man felt himself free and happy. You have been incessantly labouring to render the people discontented with their situation and dissatisfied with their form of Government, which has never been equalled since the creation, and which I am persuaded will never be excelled while the Sun and Moon shall endure." Russell goes on to accuse him: "By falsehood and misrepresentation, by the vilest artifices, you have laboured to poison the minds of the people." He says he has made Sheffield "the execration and abhorrence of the whole world"… "you be a most pernicious, you are also a most contemptible animal; a rat may burn a royal dock-yard; a mad dog unchained and unmuzzled may do much mischief, but you and your associates say you only aim at reform… I charge you and your faction with aiming, not at reforming but subverting and destroying the constitution… I charge you with labouring to introduce universal suffrage; or in other

words, for the lowest and most indigent classes of society (and three fourths of every community must necessarily consist of such) to dictate laws to, and dispose of the property of, all superior Orders of the State."

(This was the Church and King party showing their true colours. The men of property feared democracy. Another letter of his in the *Courant* in December bemoans the fact that: "The poor, maintained by all the parishes in the kingdom, are far more numerous than all the capital merchants and gentlemen of landed property of £100 a year, and upwards; of course the former would have far greater weight in the choice of representatives. Servants, Labourers, common manufacturers, and mechanics, men of little or no property, are, at least, five times more numerous than all the people of property in the kingdom: of consequence they would have five times more weight in the national assembly.")

Gales replied to Russell's attack in the next *Register* in a brief and dignified manner stating that he refutes every charge advanced against him but chooses not to reply at length as "*The Register* is too valuable to the public and my time to my family to be engrossed by you." He cannot resist adding however that the language of Russell's letter is "as remote from the character of a gentleman as the sentiment which dictated it is contrary to the spirit of charity, which as a minister of the Gospel of peace you ought to possess and inculcate."

The Constitutional Society also published the following resolution in Gales defence:

"The Sheffield Register deserves the respect, support and encouragement of this Society, and every friend to freedom and reform, as a truly independent, impartial, patriotic and well-conducted paper; and that the members of this Society will, to the utmost of their power, both in a collective and individual capacity, use their utmost endeavours to promote the general interests and welfare of the worthy proprietor and editor of the same."

They also commissioned a detailed response to Russell from one of their members, the ebullient Enoch Trickett who was less circumspect in his comments. His lengthy letter concludes:

> "We are obliged to you for the intimation you give in your postscript, that you mean to vent more poisonous venom under the signature of 'Observator.' Frequent evacuations from so filthy a fountain, may, perhaps, in time, somewhat clear the stream – though we despair of it being ever entirely purified. We are only sorry for the poor printers, who are to be so often exposed to the contagion of so infected and pestilential an atmosphere as must result from so much morbid matter being deposited in so small a circumference as a printing room."

A "furious party spirit" indeed!

Guillotines, Fifes, Drums and Bullets

The King of France had been executed in January 1793 and the autumn saw large numbers of executions of aristocrats in France including the French Queen. These events are reported in *The Sheffield Register* and roundly condemned. There is no attempt to gloss over or excuse the atrocities. However, the reports in *The Register* bracket the death of the queen with the execution of the defending garrison at Toulon by the invading British forces which are similarly condemned, and the report on the death of the aristocrats is accompanied by the posing of a question: to what extent should Britain be considered complicit in their deaths, given that propaganda linked to the invasion encouraged them to resist and rebel against the French government?

Despite attempts by Gales and others to raise such questions and point to the parallels, the revulsion in Britain against these executions helped the government to gain support for what initially had been a widely unpopular war and also to play on the anxieties of the more prosperous classes that unless a firm line was taken against lower class radicals similar atrocities could take place in Britain. Upper and middle class support for the reformist causes was weakened. An indicator of this was the decision by the Yorkshire MP Wilberforce to formally withdraw his sponsorship of *The Sheffield Register* (replaced by Charles Grey). On some other issues such as the abolition of the slave trade Wilberforce was a determined champion of reform and his action highlights the extent to which those who were working for extension of the franchise for parliamentary elections were becoming increasingly marginalized, as the wedge was driven home.

In September when Vice-admiral, Lord Hood recaptured Toulon it became an excuse for celebrations by the Church and King party to spill over into intimidation of reformists. *The Register* did not celebrate. Gales saw it as an prolongation of the war, and an ongoing cost to the public purse of a million pounds a year in ships and a garrison of 5,000 men: "We cannot here omit to reprobate the practice of collecting together large bodies of men, to express either joy or to the contrary." Referring to the use of recruiting parties, with fife and drum, and firing of cannon as part of the celebrations he comments; "Such proceedings excite disgust in persons of opposite sentiments, and dreadful disorder might have been the result, in the present instance (as an opposition party was soon assembled more formidable than the cannoneers) were not the general spirit of the people of Sheffield, PEACE. We wish that similar bodies of men may not in future be gathered together on such an occasion, nor that money should be circulated to promote inebriety and therefore hazard the harmony and happiness of the town."

This is only half the story. There is an account in Holland and Everett taken from a letter Gales wrote to a friend. What happened was that a mob, accompanied by a recruiting party with fife and drum, surrounded Gales house threatening to break the windows. His friends responded: "…an hour later upwards of a hundred stout democrats stood before us singing *God Save Great Thomas Paine* to the loyal tune. This party increased to 500 and paraded the streets peaceably (except singing) all the day. Nor would they leave till they apprehended all danger to be past."

He adds: "I do not think a riot can be managed in this place: this was apparently a push for one" adding the wry comment: "You see what it is to be supported."

The Sheffield Courant laments the rejoicings being marred: "we are sorry to say, all were not of one mind, for the disaffected party (tho' of no consequence) were disagreeably conspicuous."

The *Courant* also goes on to try to ridicule Gales following an incident on the previous Saturday when following a defeat of the armies combined against the French someone fired a shot in celebration from out of a window of the *Register* building. They don't let the truth get in the way of a good story and imply the subject was Gales himself: "A certain Jacobin Knight of the Bodkin, was so elated with the tidings, that he loaded his musquet, and discharged the same from the window of his shop; the muzzle of the piece being unluckily placed not more than two inches out of the window, the effect of it were confined within the room, which being a garret, and of a slight building, the explosion shiver'd nine squares of glass to atoms. The disaster operated so strongly upon the soul of the valiant snip, (who was apprehensive the roof was coming upon him) that he fell down speechless, and it was some time before returning signs of life appeared; proper means being used he was at last brought to himself, and the only serious consequence resulting from his ridiculous exultation, is that of discharging the glazier's bill."

Gales account is rather more measured, conscious of the fact that British troops were among the slain: "We were concerned to hear a number of guns fired on Saturday, on receiving the news of the disastrous affair before Dunkirk as that event was certainly a cause of extreme sorrow for this country: except, indeed, we were assured, that the loss of so many brave men, of so many cannon, and so much ammunition, would have an effect to close an expensive and calamitous war: and in this case, it would be much more wise and becoming to rejoice in private. Otherwise, who that acknowledges Man as his Brother, could rejoice at events written in blood, and marked with horror?" His footnote confirms the report that a gun was fired from the Gales' house, which he describes as "an indecent and unbecoming act." He goes on: "a piece was fired two or three times by one of the boys in the printing office early in the morning, for which he was reprimanded."

∽ঙ৯∽

Persecution Cannot Make Us Converts

In August, Thomas Muir, a gifted Scottish Reform leader, was sentenced to 14 years transportation in Edinburgh after being found guilty of seditious libel in what was little more than a sham trial. The charge related to the circulation of literature advocating parliamentary reform, including that of Paine, and *The Patriot*, a journal of reformist writings, printed by Gales. Then in September an English Unitarian minister, Thomas Fyshe Palmer, working in Scotland was sentenced to seven years transportation for writing an address against the war. Gales includes factual reports of the trials in *The Sheffield Register* posing the question: "Do not our readers think this verdict like Muir's a severe one? And does it not strike at the root of free enquiry." There is no other comment.

In November he reports on the "National Convention" called in Edinburgh as an act of defiance, to which English reformers were invited to send delegates in solidarity. The Scottish delegates were joined by Joseph Gerrald and Maurice Margarot from the London Corresponding Society, a reformist grouping in the capital. Matthew Campbell Browne, the editor of the *The Patriot*, represented Sheffield.

The Courant, charming as ever, uses the following wording to describe the Browne' s involvement: "The sending of the Pig of Knowledge as a delegate to the Scotch convention, is further proof of the *wonderful wisdom and sagacity* of the Swinish Multitude, and no doubt, but he will acquit himself in such a manner as to give that *learned body* no reason to repent of their election. At his return, (if ever that should be) some signal mark of the herd's approbation, will surely be conferred upon him."

The Register reports on the break up of the convention by the Lord Provost and his officers and the arrest of delegates and the

Scottish secretary of the Friends of the People, William Skirving. The subsequent trials of Margarot, Gerrald and Skirving are also reported.

In a way they fell into a trap. As the law stood in 1793 in England, the ruling classes had a dilemma when it came to strangling reform: they had a choice between indicting someone for high treason or the lesser charge of seditious libel, which gave all the powers to the jury. The only other course was summary trial by local magistrates. None of these were sufficiently robust or reliable to strike the sort of terror into dissenters needed to kill off the movement. Scottish law, however, was different: judges were more pliable and juries could be selected.

In these trials use of the words "citizen" and "convention" were adduced as proof of seditious intent. Skirving attempted to object to the inclusion of government "pensioners and placemen" on the jury but he was overruled. All three were found guilty and sentenced to 14 years transportation. Gerrald and Skirving died within a year of being transported and only Margarot returned alive to Britain. Commenting on Margarot's trial in January 1794 Gales writes: "Persecution cannot persuade the understanding even when it subdues the resolution. It may make us hypocrites but it cannot make us converts."

In the same edition he notes that Browne was not yet indicted. Browne never was charged or brought to trial. The Montgomery memoir says that: "Of the fidelity of this man to the cause of the reformers, Montgomery did not, from the first, entertain a high opinion; and it was not strengthened by a reference to the facts that, while it was well known that he played so conspicuous a part in the meetings of the "Convention," he was never, in any way, called to account by the public prosecutor, nor did he ever return to Sheffield to answer for his proceedings to those who sent him to, and maintained him in, Scotland."

Quite what this means is not clear from the available records. Gales, in a letter to a friend Joseph Aston (quoted in the Montgomery memoir) said at the time: "Poor Brown's is a hard fate; but his spirits are excellent—so are the spirits of all the sufferers. There is something in persecution so fine, so invigorating that those who suffer under it never want spirits." He adds: "The present is a dark period; no man can penetrate the gloom." He is named as a Government witness in state trials, and it appears that he somehow came to an agreement with the authorities to avoid prosecution.

Gerrald was the last to be tried and sentenced and in March Gales prints a lengthy summary of his defence which he conducted himself, praising his oratory. Gerrald informed the court that he had declined to act on the advice of his friends to forfeit his bail and flee the country as he could not "relinquish the cause," which he put as: "Whether man is to be permitted to exercise the power of reason; or by prohibiting him from doing so, extinguish every great and noble qualification of his nature?" He continued – referring as did many reformers to the revolution of 1688 – "The word *innovation* alarms us, but let us attend to it. – What is all reform but innovation? – Was not the Revolution an innovation? – Was not the Reformation an innovation? Was not the Christian Religion itself an innovation? [*Here the court interrupted him for speaking in such an indecent manner*]" Commenting on the verdicts and sentences E. P. Thompson writes that though Scottish judges were docile or partisan, and juries could be picked with impunity, these verdicts could not be considered maverick as they were wholeheartedly endorsed by Pitt and other members of his government and supporters, including Wilberforce. He adds that the revulsion of feeling among decent respectable Englishmen was such that the rate of acquittals by English juries increased.

Local news and Comment 1793 - 1794

The prominence given to issues such as parliamentary reform and the opposition to the war, did not result in a reduction in the coverage of local issues. At the end of 1793 Gales had increased the size of the newspaper, without raising the price, so that this could be avoided. He continued to report on and commend instances of philanthropy whether institutional or private. The Rotherham Benevolent Society is praised for its work in relief of poverty and he notes that within the course of twelve months 124 persons had received assistance.

Elsewhere he tells how a lady from Ireland visiting the city had gone to see the prisoners in the gaol and after asking the keeper for details of the numbers and ages of children of the inmates had paid off the debts of two such in full thus enabling their release.

A story similar to one from earlier, heavy with condemnatory satire, occurs in the newspaper on 12th July 1793:

> "This morning was sold by public auction, and delivered in the public market, to the highest bidder, a useful piece of *Household Furniture*, called a WIFE, late the property of Linley Pilley, which with a good hempen necklace, fetched no less a sum – than one shilling! – How amazingly has this necessary of life fallen in price since last week; a piece of the same earthenware having been then sold, as is positively affirmed, for nineteen guineas! – N.B. It is perhaps necessary to inform our readers, that a slip of paper, in the shape of a promissory note for £100 by the lady's father, which was in her pocket, considerably enhanced her intrinsic value!!! – Will this not furnish business for the gentlemen of the bar?"

Nothing that concerned the welfare of the city was too small scale for his attention. He commented on the dirty state of the streets and urged the Court Leet to appoint another street cleaner or "scavenger" as they were called at the time. Elsewhere he reported on an altercation between the Master Cutler and two Quakers recently appointed to the Cutlers' Company when the latter refused to remove their hats in the Cutlers Hall.

Relating to the commercial life of the city there were a number of reports about meetings to plan or promote new canals in the neighbourhood, including a meeting to initiate a subscription for the extension of the canal from Tinsley to Sheffield at which £8600 was pledged.

One of the most interesting crime stories concerns the overturning of a horse driven coach by dangerous driving:

"Yesterday fe'nnight in the evening a melancholy accident happened by the overturning of the new Doncaster coach, at the entrance to this town. The coach was full of passengers, all of whom escaped unhurt, except a Mr Stones (who had lately removed from Tickhill to this place – and, it is said was looking out of the coach window at the moment) who was killed on the spot. The Coroner's inquest was called over the body on Saturday; but its decision was adjourned to Monday, when the jury brought a verdict *Manslaughter* against the coachmen who drives to the Angel Inn, in this place – it having appeared in evidence that he repeatedly crossed the road of the new coach and otherwise annoyed it, with his empty carriage, so as at length to cause it to be overturned, whereby Mr Stones was unfortunately killed. – The man was accordingly committed to the castle of York to take his trial at the ensuing Assizes. – This shocking catastrophe, we hope, will have a salutary effect, in connecting the shameful and dangerous practice to which coachmen are too prone, of striving for the poor pre-eminence of being the first in town..."

It would seem that boy racers were not unknown in the late eighteenth century.

The Register also continued to report social events, unlike its sister reformist newspaper the *Manchester Herald*, which in an advert inserted into *The Register* announced its declared policy of omitting such reports. Gales, or possibly Winifred, wrote of such events with a flourish. The following example is not untypical:

"On Thursday evening a most elegant and sumptuous entertainment was given at the new coffee house in George Street. The supper did great credit to the exertions of Mr and Mrs Hardcastle, and the whole was conducted in very superior style. The staircase and ballroom was illuminated with variegated lamps, displayed with great taste in different forms. The amusements commenced with a concert to which succeeded dancing, cards and billiards. One hundred and forty ladies and gentlemen were present and time winged its flight so rapidly that it was four o clock in the morning before they departed."

The fact that the newspaper retained such a broad coverage of local stories may be a key reason why its circulation continued to grow despite the extent to which Gales was increasingly vilified by some sections of opinion in the town. In December 1793 he claimed it had exceeded a circulation of 1900, and by April the following year it had reached 2025 despite the harassment of vendors in some neighbouring towns.

❦❦

Burst Every Dungeon, Every Chain - February 28th 1794

In February 1794, another general fast day was called by the government. Again there was a defiant meeting of reformists, not supportive of the jingoistic intent. On March 6th *The Sheffield Register* contained the following report of this mass meeting, held in an open piece of ground in West Street:

> "Friday, being the day appointed for a general fast, was particularly observed in this town; as, notwithstanding the day was rather wet, between five and six thousand persons, who did not approve of the service provided by the authority for the occasion, or of the usual ceremonies for such days, held a solemn public meeting in the open air, and attended to a serious lecture, written by a labouring mechanic, but nevertheless suitable to their own ideas of propriety, which was preceded by a prayer, and concluded by an hymn (a copy of which will be found on the last page) and the passing of the resolutions advertised in the preceding column. The business over, every man went peaceably home."

The hymn was written by James Montgomery and takes the form of
a prayer to God to further the cause of Liberty and Peace. The first
and last verses are:

'O God of Hosts, thine ear incline,
Regards our prayers, our cause is thine:
When orphans cry, when babes complain
When widows weep, canst Thou refrain?

Burst every dungeon, every chain,
Give injured slaves their rights again;
Let truth prevail, let discord cease,
Speak – and the world shall smile in peace'

The resolutions included:
-   A condemnation of the war which is termed a war of
    "combined kings" against the people of France,
-   An assertion that public fasts linked to support for the
    shedding of "oceans of human blood" are solemn
    prostitutions of religion,
-   A concern that the landing in England of Hessian
    mercenaries "a ferocious and unprincipled horde of
    Butchers" has a "suspicious and alarming appearance"
    especially in view of the erection of barracks throughout the
    country – "an introductory means of filling them with
    foreign mercenaries,"
-   A declaration that the people need to be on their guard in
    view of the above,
-   A vote of thanks to the Earl of Stanhope for his speech in
    support of the "suffering patriots," Muir, Palmer, Skirving
    and Margarot,
-   A declaration of intent to continue to press for a reform of
    parliament even though "we follow our brethren in the
    same glorious cause to Botany Bay."

The resolutions illustrate the prevalent mood of distrust and
apprehension and the depth of alienation from their government

and King. They also show how the Sheffield people were well informed about national events as a result of the content and availability of *The Sheffield Register*.

Sheffield was not unique in holding such mass meetings. They were held in other towns around that time including London. They served to maintain the morale and motivations of the embattled reformist elements among the people at a time when oppression was being systematically heightened by the government and their supporters.

Further evacuations from the filthy fountain that was the Rev. John Russell followed in the *Courant*. He describes it as an assembly for the vile purposes of sedition and treason, a gathering of "Frenchified traitors, men who are enemies of the King, of the Constitution, of their Country, of the Laws, of Liberties and Property of England; men who will be ready to join their frantic French brethren, whenever an opportunity shall arise." There is not any part of the Kingdom that shall read the account alluded to, but will at once exclaim 'if this be true, Sheffield ought to be laid in ashes.' " He then goes on to make what could justifiably call an incitement to criminality and violence, such as had been seen in many other towns: "Inhabitants of Sheffield, your tame pusillanimity is highly blameable; there is not another town in the kingdom that would have suffered such an insult to be offered to it. Will you suffer yourselves to be thus tamely insulted, and the character of your town to be vilified and degraded in the eyes of the whole nation by a despicable handful of vile traitors? Rouze, instantly rouze yourselves to manly and spirited exertions."

A New Meteor Flares

When a young man called Henry Yorke appeared on the scene towards the end of 1792, Winifred describes the moment as a "new meteor flaring on the political horizon." He first came to the attention of the Galeses through a pamphlet he wrote on the abolition of the slave trade. He came to Sheffield as a delegate of the Derby Constitutional Society.

Winifred says his manners were "so gentlemanly, his conversation so highly interesting, and his acquirements so extraordinary that everyone was fascinated with him. On his first visit his stay was short, but he attended all the public meetings, and a general anxiety was evinced for his return. At this period, his discussion of the great national question was moderately couched; was rational and important, and his experiences enabled him to throw new light on the subject, and he was considered a powerful auxiliary."

His charisma was clearly very powerful, "so eloquent he was, few could withstand his bold assertions." This can be in no doubt – you only have to read the transcript of his conduct of his own defence in his later trial, in 1795, to appreciate his way with words. These qualities made him dangerous in the eyes of the establishment. He faced a charge of conspiracy against the government in June 1793, but was found not guilty. He went on trial again, this time at Lancaster assizes in August for misdemeanours according to the *Register*: "since the charge of High Treason could not be established." Winifred says that when he returned from the Scottish Convention, he had assumed "a higher tone." Moderate men (presumably referring to Joseph and others in her circle, including herself): "were afraid that this admired orator would influence the public mind, and endeavoured to abate the warmth of the general feeling."

Joseph Gales, however, clearly seems to have, on one occasion at least, been carried away with the "warmth of general feeling" when he wrote of the Castle Hill meeting: "we had a capital meeting: I had the honour to be drawn along with Yorke amidst the thousands."

There is another interesting side to Yorke – he was mixed race. His father was Samuel Redhead, an agent for the owners of the island of Barbuda in the Caribbean, and himself a sugar plantation owner. Yorke's mother was a slave.

That this eloquent, dark-skinned, English gentleman was a bit of a crowd-puller is perhaps not surprising. There was no doubt a fascination amongst the 18th century public for the "otherness" of the man – the exotic. It is hard from this distance to determine how much attitudes to race played a part in this. It is possible to read disdain into the words that James Montgomery wrote some time afterwards, though this may be just a 21st century reading: "He was if not a mulatto, a quadroon – a fiery orator, and, as I thought, in the habit of delivering as his own, portions of the impassioned speeches of Mirabeau; his style was altogether French. His figure, when he appeared at the Castle Hill meeting, was good, and his dress striking, if not the best taste – with Hessian Boots and a stock of republican plainness; he wore a silk coat and a waistcoat of court fashion; his hair at the same time defying the curt French character by its luxuriant curl – a tendency derived from the sunny side of his ancestral tree."

He was sent to England in 1778 at the age of 6 to be educated, and after Cambridge University was admitted to the Inner Temple in 1790; but his career as a reformist orator took over. Winifred also said that the young Henry Yorke was taken under the wing of Edmund Burke and accompanied him on a tour in revolutionary France.

Yorke was the last of those tried for treason to face trial – after Hardy and the others were acquitted by juries not convinced enough to send someone to the gallows, Yorke's charge was downgraded to one of seditious conspiracy in order to a stand a better chance of securing a conviction.

◈

Castle Hill – April 1794

An even larger gathering than that in February was held on the 7th April 1794 at Castle Hill, and the tone of this meeting was more strident – bordering on defiance. This in part was probably due to the effect of the principal orator Henry Yorke sent to support the Sheffield Society by the Derby Constitutional Society. The following is an extract from *The Register*'s report of this meeting:

"Mr Yorke spoke upon the different subjects for at least two hours, in a manner so masterly and eloquent as to surprise and captivate his hearers, who were from ten to twelve thousand in number, though the day was rainy; but, notwithstanding the largeness of the company, so great were his exertions and so close the attention paid to him that there was scarcely a person present who did not distinctly hear: many, indeed, we are told, who were not heretofore remarkable for their liberality of sentiment have acknowledged themselves greatly enlightened by what they heard. – To shew the high sense entertained of Mr Yorke's services at this meeting, by the populace, he was no sooner seated in the coach which attended on him, than the horses were taken from the carriage, and the people drew him through most of the public streets in Sheffield amid the acclamation of thousands; – which done, after a few admonitory words from the orator every man went peaceably home.'

The resolutions passed at the meeting included:
-   That the People were the true and only source of government.
-   That the sentences on Muir, Gerrald, Skirving, Margarot and Palmer were acts better suited to the maxims of a despotic than a free government.
-   Endorsement of an address to the King requesting their pardon.
-   A declaration that equality of representation in Parliament should be demanded as a right not petitioned as a favour and a resolution that they would petition no more on this issue.
-   A resolution to petition the King on the total abolition of slavery – not just the slave trade
-   A decision to send a congratulatory letter to Thomas Walker of Manchester on his acquittal in a recent trial for high treason,
-   A vote of thanks to all the English juries who refused to find guilty their fellow citizens brought to trial for speaking what they thought.

The wording of the petition to the King on the abolition of slavery contained the following passages:

> 'As intellectual beings we conceive it to be a sacred obligation, imposed on us by the Supreme Being to think for ourselves.'
> 'Wishing to be rid of the weight of oppression under which we groan, we are induced to compassionate those who groan also, and to desire an alleviation of their sufferings.'
> ' —we cannot call ourselves free men in the strict sense of the word: Yet our lives cannot be taken from us but for crimes previously defined and declared punishable by law; nor can our persons be wantonly used to gratify the lust, the avarice, or the cruelty of overseers and slave drivers. So far we have undoubtedly have an advantage over the negro Slaves.'

Henry Yorke's speech was printed by the Galeses and sold from the shop – its wording was dissected and was a central feature at his subsequent trial.

Thomas Walker's reply to the letter of congratulation sent to him also contains some interesting passages. It was printed in *The Sheffield Register* on April 17th. He welcomes the "approbation of the upright and intelligent part of my countrymen."

He expresses his relief: "Notwithstanding all the malignity exerted against us, the event has proved that we had nothing to fear in relying on our innocence and the integrity of an English Jury."

He comments: "Thank God we are not arrived in England at the point of arbitrary jurisprudence which for mere opinions has consigned Messrs Muir, Palmer, Skirving, Margarot, and Gerrald to transportation like felons, to the dreary and miserable climate of Botany Bay – may your application in their behalf meet the success which its justice demands; and may the true spirit of English law never be contaminated by punishments so utterly disproportioned even to the alleged offence"

Earlier in the letter he had nevertheless acknowledged that the outcome of his trial had been precarious. He states that bribery was the means by which the evidence had been obtained and the lies of the witness had been so comprehensively exposed that he was charged with perjury, but Walker acknowledged that if a second such witness had been procured, and if it has not been possible to refute all the false evidence, the outcome could have been less favourable. As well as being proprietor of the *Manchester Herald*, Walker was a prosperous industrialist who could afford to commission the best defence counsel available: Thomas Erskine.

A Last Roll of the Dice – Impertinence and Illiberality

E. P. Thompson comments on the establishment of volunteer corps throughout the country in 1794 fuelled by "war fever" in some sections of the community. The declared purpose of these bodies was to be part of defence of the country against a possible French invasion, the risk of which was grossly exaggerated by the government to mobilise support for the war. On May 1st, in the same edition in which he reports record sales of 2025 copies, Gales ascribes an entirely different objective to the establishment of the Sheffield corps:

> "It would be a miracle indeed, if during the present rage for battle and murder, certain inhabitants of Sheffield were outstripped in quixotic loyalty by any town in England. A number of heroes have accordingly agreed to form themselves into a military corps, to be called *The Independent Sheffield Volunteers*; to be armed, accoutred, clothed and disciplined at their own expense, with the charitable intention, we are told, of being ready, when *required*, to embrue their hands in the blood of those of their fellow townsmen who are so audaciously rebellious as to – SPEAK AS THEY THINK!!!"

He continues by naming the leader of the group as Mr Peech, landlord of the Angel Inn, and describes a parade through the streets with drum and fife followed chiefly by a rabble of children amid hootings and hissings. A number of working men then assembled outside the inn to express their displeasure at the proceedings after which they went peaceably home: "to the utter displeasure of certain persons." Gales saw this as another attempt to provoke a riot in order to justify heavy-handed intervention.

Winifred describes these volunteers in her memoir: "The Volunteers, who were generally young inconsiderate Men, 'proud of a little brief authority' were supported by the Civil Authorities, and assumed a mode of conduct, which to use a gentle phrase was very impertinent. These make-believe soldiers, on the strength of their Musquets scrupled not to insult the lower, but industrious part of Community, and who as they were too poor to purchase fire-arms as a mode of self-defense, furnished themselves with pikes i.e. a staff with a piece of pointed iron at the top of it."

In the same edition of 1st May, Gales prints, unedited, a letter to a private individual in Eckington which had been passed on to him and which he ironically characterises as an "elegant literary curiosity." He names the sender as a Mr S Marshall of Sheffield and says: "we give it our readers as a specimen of the liberality, veracity and good sense of that gentleman."

"Gales Has Given up his Edea of a Convention on Monday tis well he Has – He is a Vile indeed – See his paper the Last week I send you a Few wrote as Burlesque – the are Smart who the author is I don't know – when lawless landed with Redhead alias York – with Cammage & the Sec. Broomhead – He said from his Window Citizens disperse – & then Exclaimed now See how the Obey me – I have sent Last week, & this Week, papers to Earl Fitzwilliam, and Have had friendly Reply to my first Letter Tis Said Justice Bond is Coming done & more troops are Coming what Reproach this troubler in our Israel this man of the people from Eckington."

The following week Marshall writes direct to Gales complaining about his publishing the letter. Gales prints the second letter also with all its ungrammatical incoherence and spelling mistakes uncorrected.

One can only speculate on the change in emphasis, the naming of his traducers and opponents and the very forthright use of personal ridicule. He seemed to have recognised that the attempt to conduct the debate on a calm, rational and impersonal level had met with no positive response from the other side and he may have decided to attempt to subdue the intensity of their personal attacks and bravado by exposing them to their fellow citizens. One of Marshall's complaints in the second letter is about the insults and threats he had received from people who had previously showed him respect and "esteem."

But there was also a national context. And it raises the question to what extent was this a last roll of the dice? Reports on news from elsewhere in the country suggest that Gales was deeply troubled at the course events were taking and the entrenched and repressive attitudes which were becoming prevalent. For example, in his report on what he calls the "banishment" of Joseph Priestley he writes that it is "the strongest proof of the extreme illiberality and persecuting spirit of the present times, and how dangerous a thing it is to oppose an alarmed and irritated priesthood." This was written on April 17th two months before his departure and suggests that "To flee or not to flee" was already the question, though it probably took subsequent events to bring him to a firm decision.

The Net Tightens

On 12th May 1794 several prominent members of the London Corresponding Society were arrested on suspicion of high treason, including Thomas Hardy, a founder member and its first secretary. A sackful of papers was removed from Hardy's house and two days later a Committee of Secrecy was appointed by Parliament to examine the papers and interview witnesses. Further arrests were made in London and the provinces and on 24th May three members of the Sheffield Constitutional Society: William Broomhead, William Camage and Robert Moody were arrested. Broomhead was secretary to the Sheffield Society and Camage the previous secretary. *The Register* reported the Sheffield arrests on May 29th including the fact that all three were immediately conveyed to London under military escort. Further arrests in Sheffield followed.

An Act to suspend Habeas Corpus became law on 23rd May 1794. The Habeas Corpus Act had been in place since 1679 and ensured that no one could be detained without charge: so that the legality of a detention could be challenged in a court of law. In his May 29th editorial, Gales spells out the implications for his readers:

> "The Star Chamber, High Commission, and Court Martial, though arbitrary jurisdictions, yet had still some pretence of a trial, at least of a sentence; but on the suspension of the Habeas Corpus Act, not only the substance, but even the pretence of a trial, or sentence vanishes. Every person is liable by a warrant from the Secretary of State, or other of his Majesty's Ministers, to be imprisoned in any jail during any time that such Minister or other Ministers shall think proper, and let their treatment there be what it may, they are precluded from obtaining any kind of legal redress, let the injuries they suffer in their dreary mansion, be of what nature soever; and having no action for false imprisonment or malicious prosecution, they are debarred of all remedy for any damage they may sustain in their persons, character or fortunes."

Gales is critical of the large number of members of Parliament who were absent from the House when such an important measure was put through: " not one half of the House of Commons, as appears by even the largest divisions, were present. We are happy, however, to inform the public that the whole 558 members, to a man, mean to promise the most faithful and constant attendance – *at the next general election!*" He prints the act of suspension in full, and on 5th June adds the following comment:

> "Every wretch in the country, who has through malice or envy a dislike to his neighbour, will now have the opportunity of gratifying his malicious intentions. Ministers should be cautious how they commit men on light and frivolous

grounds or without proper examination. Those who have commenced spies and informers, will use little delicacy, and less truth in the information they give: and merely to shew that they are deserving of their diabolical hire, will crowd the prisons with innocent people, as long as the liberties of Englishmen are at the mercy of such debased and infamous characters!!"

This was not just scaremongering. That same month there is a report of one of their newspaper distributors, George Thompson, of New Mills, being arrested and taken directly to York Castle for selling a pamphlet. Thompson is described as "a faithful servant, a good citizen, and a good son," his arrest leaving his elderly mother without support.

A letter is printed on the 5th June by someone signing themselves "Aristocrat" – presumably to show to readers just what those who professed moderation and tolerance were up against:

"Ah, ah, ah, ah! I can but laugh, Mr Printer, (little as we inclined so to do, at present) to think how truly ridiculous you, and your swinish friends, must have appeared, when you first received the stupendous intelligence of the Parliament of Great Britain having, with that enthusiastic fervour, and patriotic precipitancy, so peculiarly characteristic of the venerable sages of the British Empire, flogged a bill through both – to suspend, sine die, that liberty which some of you might vainly have flattered yourselves the constitution could not legally have deprived you of; and given an hundredfold additional power to the sacred government of Church and State! How much you must have been thunderstruck, at our importation of so grand a part of the system of Robespierre! And how cursedly alarmed you must all been now be (as I confess is very natural) lest we should bring up the rear of the plan with the guillotine, and dispense with the control of juries, as well as the restraint of the Habeas Corpus act!"

That same week *The Register* contains a report on the proceedings of the Committee of Secrecy. One of the letters found at Hardy's house was a letter from "a person at Sheffield by profession a printer (who has since absconded)."

This letter said that "The barefaced Aristocracy of the present Administration made it necessary that we should be prepared to act on the defensive against any attack they may command their newly-armed Minions to make on us." The letter continues by informing Hardy that plan has been put together to manufacture a number of pikes made of tempered steel which can be supplied to other societies at a price of one shilling each. The letter concludes that orders should be sent to the secretary of the Sheffield Constitutional Society but adds that in the letter this was "struck through."

The report goes on to record the answers given by one of the arrested Sheffield men though not by name. He is alleged to have said that they believed that the Government was "conspiring against the people, and therefore should be resisted." Another unnamed witness interviewed claimed that he had been told by one of the persons arrested that the pikes were to be used "in case the people were to rise, for the particular purpose of keeping off the cavalry."

It was also said that on the advice of one on the London Delegates to the Convention at Edinburgh, the people of Sheffield had been convinced that as the opposite party was arming they had a right to arm too, as a matter of right, enshrined in the 1689 Bill of Rights. It was elsewhere stated that a pike was found at the house of one of the arrested Sheffield men at the time of his arrest.

The letter from Sheffield was written by a Richard Davison, an employee of the Galeses. Winfred Gales recalls the circumstances of the letter: "A young Man who belonged to the Leeds Society, came to work with us, and was appointed Corresponding Secretary to one of the Societies. In this capacity, he wrote to one of the London Agents enquiring whether they would adopt the same mode of defence which the friends of Reform in Sheffield meant to adopt. Of this act we knew nothing until the "Secret Committee" found his letter amongst Hardy's papers, dated "Gales's Printing Office.""

Joseph himself comments on the above events in his address to the people of Sheffield printed in *The Sheffield Register* on 27th June and quoted in full below. Though he denies all knowledge of the letter to Hardy it would appear that he was aware of the intention of the members of the Sheffield Society to arm themselves. It is perhaps surprising given many of his previous pronouncements that he does not appear to have counselled them against taking such steps.

❧❧❧

Flying to the Sun

The manufacture of pikes gave the government an excuse to act against Gales and other members of the Sheffield Society, even though there was only questionable hearsay evidence that they were intended for anything other than defensive purposes.

With hindsight it appears naive not to have predicted such a reaction. Gales may also have contributed to the engendering of the state of collective anxiety which prompted the decision to acquire arms through the way he reported the arrival of Hessian mercenaries in the country who he described as a "set of human butchers who gain their livelihood by cutting the throats of their fellow creatures."

Winifred comments that "public indignation was excited generally, from government having taken into pay some Hessian and Hanoverian troops. In order it is believed, to over awe and, keep guard over people, as it would be difficult to make native soldiers act against them."

But, given other events of 1794, it is understandable that many felt that there was a real risk of the foreign mercenaries being used against the British people. The subsequent way that volunteer corps were deployed in Sheffield (at Norfolk Street) and the subsequent Peterloo massacre in Manchester, suggests grounds for concern were not that fanciful.

Also the *Register* carries a report on the 14th June of the arrests of two men, Lindley and Warrior, for firing pistols or muskets into the open windows of a man called Jonathan Leadbeater, at whose house lodged three compositors on the newspaper. Their defence was that those inside were "Gales' men" and a witness was produced who said that Leadbeater had "damned the king." The magistrate

Athorpe, treating them lightly, released the men without requiring bail for future behaviour and bound them over to the next Rotherham Sessions.

At the trial of Yorke, attempts were made to get witnesses to admit that disturbances were being planned in Sheffield, and that Yorke's speech was an incitement to armed insurrection, but a consistent message emerges, perhaps best summed up in a few words from the cross examination of William Broomhead:

"You have had no disturbance at Sheffield?"

"No; they cannot make us do it at Sheffield; we know better."

"Did you consider that speech a peaceable speech, and not tending in any manner to the reverse?"

"I did; it was never in Mr Yorke's power, or anybody else has to attempt to breed disturbances."

"Did he attempt it?"

"No; if he had, it would not have been in his power to have it done."

Another witness, a committee member of the Constitutional Society, under cross examination by the prosecution has these questions put to him:

"Did not anybody think of reproaching Mr Gales for selling in his shop a thing that was a scandalous account of his friend's speech?"

"I do not know that anybody did."

"You did not reprove him for it?"

"No."

"And you never made any complaint about it?"

"No."

"Do not you think he was a gross libeller in putting out such a thing?"

"Go along, man, it is impossible to believe a word you say."

Further insight into the mentality and prevailing mood in the town can be obtained from Thomas Hardy's trial for treason in the autumn of 1794 (*Howell's State Trials*). Broomhead was asked about the constitutional society and whether anyone in it had an idea of making an attack on the king or the House of Lords. Broomhead replied: "I think they ought to be sent to Bedlam, if they had." And when he was asked about if he had any intention of such an attack he said: "Just the same as flying to the sun."

Another member of the Sheffield society, Henry Hill, a cutler, explained their reason for preparing the pikes:

"From the opposite party using such threats, even in the dead of the night, they have come where I lodged and insulted us of a night when we have been in bed, and have sworn they would pull down the house and burn it, calling us Jacobins… They have even shot into people's houses, an armed set of people that made a parade in the street; and when going home at twelve o'clock at night, they shot under a person's door."

"This was an armed set of people at Sheffield?"

"They procured arms and paraded the street, and if there was any great victory gained—"

"Upon some occasion of this sort, they fired through or under one of the doors?"

"They did."

"Was it this sort of conduct, and those threats, that induced you first to prepare arms?"

"No other thing, no other view."

It seems it was acceptable to the authorities to carry guns if you were on the right side, but treasonable to even possess a pike if you were on the side threatening their hold on power (and wealth).

Slipping the Net

There is some mystery over the whereabouts of Joseph Gales at this time. The "pikes" letter gave the authorities the excuse they needed to move to arrest Gales, Yorke and Davidson for treason.

Jewitt says that when "the Habeas Corpus Act was suspended a warrant was issued for his apprehension and he had only time to escape by the back door and to make his way in the middle of the night to the house of a friend, I think of the name of Needham in Chesterfield where he remained concealed for some weeks until an opportunity offered for the passage over to America."

The account in the Holland and Everett book is that Henry Yorke had contrived to obtain the affections of Gales' youngest sister, Sarah, and that Yorke left for Derby "in an unsatisfactory manner, so far as his intentions towards the lady were concerned; and to that town, after having published his newspaper on the 16th March, Gales followed him. In the course of they day, a government messenger, accompanied by the local constable, entered the house of the Sheffield printer with a warrant for his arrest on a charge of conspiracy!

Winifred herself does refer to Joseph being away at Derby when Habeas Corpus was suspended (though she is clearly confused as she put in brackets "Mr Payne's of New Hill" – which was at Wath). She goes on to say that messages were sent to him urging him to stay away for a day or two. She describes travelling 18 miles to see him on horseback, and then going to London and Harwich via Eckington to bid farewell to his parents and to Newark to see Winifred's mother.

In a letter to the *Sheffield Independent* in 1848, Montgomery sheds some light on what happened. He says that Gales had gone to Derby on some family affairs without any personal apprehension for his safety at that time. It was while he was away that they came to his house. (This ties in with Winifred's account of dealing with the house being searched.) He says of Gales; "it required all the violence of earnest and affectionate persuasion to induce him to take refuge elsewhere."

Montgomery also tells of what happened to Davison: which he describes as happening on the same day that Broomhead, Camage et al. were arrested (this is also probably the same day they moved for Gales and Yorke i.e. May not March – probably a mistake in the Holland and Everett account). It is worth repeating the story in Montgomery's words; "two of the Sheffield constables entered a well-known public house, suddenly and bolting into the company rooms, crowded with ale-bibbers and tobacco smokers – they asked if Davison was there . He was; but the person who sat next to him, with a presence of mind and promptitude of impudence rarely exemplified, at once answered: "No; he went off to Leeds this morning." They took his word and their departure as promptly. The object of their search was from Leeds. He afterwards escaped to America where he became a store-keeper and justice of the peace."

Piecing all this together, it seems likely that Joseph Gales was not at home at the time of the suspension of Habeas Corpus, that he did escape by being out of town in Derby and that from there he travelled over to New Hill/Wath and remained in hiding. It seems that it was Winfred and Montgomery who kept the *Register* going with whatever input they could get from Joseph via messages and the occasional visit.

Winifred says: "Contemplate my dear children, the trying situation of your Mother. My husband gone! A printing office with 16 hands in it – a newspaper to edit – a store in full business – four infant, i.e. very young children, and myself within a few months of adding another to the number!" Contemplate indeed, and you will realise just how much a part of this partnership she was.

Gales' farewell to Sheffield

His farewell address to the people of Sheffield was included in the final edition of the Register on 27th June 1794:

> "After having lived ten years in Sheffield, and in habits of friendship with many respectable families in the town and neighbourhood, it is a painful task to bid them and my friends at large a serious, and perhaps eternal farewell. The disagreeable predicament in which I stand from the suspension of the Habeas Corpus Act precludes me the happiness of staying among you my friends, unless I would expose myself to the malice, enmity and power of an unjust aristocracy. It is in these persecuting days, a sufficient crime to have printed a newspaper which has boldly dared to doubt the infallibility of ministers, and to investigate the justice and policy of their measures.
>
> Could my imprisonment, or even death, serve the cause

which I have espoused – the cause of Peace, Liberty, and Justice, it would be cowardice to flee from it, but convinced that ruining my family and distressing my friends, by risking either, would only gratify the ignorant and the malignant, I shall seek that livelihood in another State which I cannot peaceably obtain in this. To be accused is, now, to be guilty, and however conscious I may be of having neither done, said, or written, any thing that militates against peace, order or good government, yet, when I am told that witnesses are suborned to swear me guilty of treasonable and seditious practices, it becomes prudent to avoid such dark assassins and leave to the informers and their employers the mortification of knowing, that however deep their villainy was planned, it has been unsuccessful.

My friends, and many I gratefully acknowledge I have found, since my residence amongst you, will do justice to my actions, and the motives which impelled them – my enemies will, as they have hitherto done, misconstrue my intentions, misinterpret my actions, and exaggerate my failings, but in the calm impartial moment of separation, I would tell them, with the firmness of conscious rectitude, that I dare any man, or set of men, to prove, even in a single instance, that I voluntarily injured an individual or deviated from that strict line of moral rectitude which marks the honest man and the useful member of society. I am accused of the heinous faults of having been a member of the Constitutional Society – I was a member of the Society of this place, and shall never, I am persuaded, whatever may be the final result, regret it, knowing and believing that the real, as well as ostensible object of this Society was a rational and peaceable reform in the representation of the people in Parliament.

I know the principles of the Society to be, generally speaking, those of peace and goodwill to all mankind; and I have never heard a sentiment, as coming from the Society, which was inimical to the purest system of peace, honesty, and good order. The Secret Committee have imputed to the Society intentions of which they had no conception, and

crimes which they abhor. The peaceable manner in which
they conducted their meetings, their conduct as a public body,
their avowed and open mode of proceeding, must evince the
injustice of the constructions put upon their intentions. None
but venal, unjust, or profligate minds, can so far pervert the
principles of the Society, as to impute to them a wish to
overturn the present form of government. They published
their intentions to arm for self-defence, and the internal safety
of the kingdom; they avowed their motives, and they
vindicated their pretensions from a clause in the Bill of
Rights, that great bulwark of British freedom, which the
suspension of the Habeas Corpus Act goes so nearly to sap. It
was natural, that poor men, and of that description are the
major part of the Society, should seek such arms as their
circumstances would afford. And, even the purchase of pikes
was more than their finances would admit of, as appears by
the very few manufactured.

It has been insinuated, and, I believe, pretty generally
believed, that I wrote the letter which is referred to by the
Secret Committee, concerning the pikes, and given in the last
Register. This charge, in the most unequivocal manner, I deny.
I neither wrote, dictated, or was privy to it; nor, till Mr
Hardy's apprehension, had I any knowledge of it. As far as
this stigma personally respects myself or my family, I am
indifferent as to the report, but I owe, to my friends and the
public, the duty to clear myself from this imputation.

It will always be my pride, that I have printed an impartial
and truly independent newspaper, and that I have done my
endeavours, humble and limited as they have been, to rescue
my countrymen from the darkness of ignorance, and to
awaken them to a full sense of their privileges as human
beings, and, as such, of their importance in the grand scale of
creation. That I have intended well, however inadequate my
exertions have been to my wishes, will be a consolation to me
when far removed from the many friendly and dear
connections I have formed in this country. Filled with every
kind sentiment towards those who wish me well, and bearing

no enmity to those who wish otherwise, I bid farewell to my numerous and steady friends; and grateful for every past favour, whether continued to the present moment, or withdrawn from political motives, I remain, wishing every honest man, whatever his political or religious sentiments may be, health, peace and comfort.

JOSEPH GALES

The address reads more as a self-justification than an explanation. At the time of writing it, Gales would have been conscious of the stands taken by Gerrald and Walker and their refusal to take the advice of friends to flee the country and avoid trial. Both made this an issue of personal honour and it would have cost Gales to take the contrary decision given his own keen sense of honour expressed in earlier editorials. The suspension of Habeas Corpus had taken place subsequent to the trials of Gerrald and Walker and he gives this as the key reason for his own decision. But the content of the address suggests that the intelligence that false witnesses had already been bribed ("suborned") to testify against him on the charges of sedition and treason was an equally important consideration particularly in view of the use of such in Walker's prosecution and Walker's own acknowledgement that if more than one such witness had been procured he might have found it difficult to convince the jury of his innocence.

Henry Yorke's Fate

Henry Yorke also left Sheffield to escape arrest, and was possibly at Derby at the time. Winifred's account of his final capture was that he had "secreted himself on the banks of the Humber, opposite Hull, and there used to amuse himself by sailing in a small skiff which lay at the beach and which he used to unmoor at pleasure. On one of his aquatic excursions, he saw a boat approach which he could not avoid, the experienced oarsman, bearing down upon him." She gives the following account of the conversation that followed:

'What is your name?'

'Melville, why do you ask?'

'No! you are Redhead Yorke, I knew by your eyes, for a lady so well described them that I cannot be mistaken.'

'Who was the dear creature who so kindly observed me? I hope she was young and beautiful!'

Yorke's subsequent trial is detailed in *Howell's State Trials*.

He was indicted along with (in absentia) Joseph Gales and Richard Davison.

The indictment is lengthy: several pages of carefully crafted prose. This is just a flavour of the key parts. It accuses them of: "being malicious, seditious, and ill-disposed persons... and maliciously and seditiously contriving and intending to break and disturb the peace and tranquillity of this realm... and did combine, conspire and confederate with each other to defame the Commons' House of Parliament and initiate a spirit of discontent, disaffection and sedition in the minds of the liege subjects of the King... and to rise and excite riots, commotions and tumults therein... and to invite and encourage the said subjects to furnish and provide arms and offensive weapons... to the evil example of all others, in the like case offending, and against the peace of our said lord the King, his crown and dignity.

The trial transcript in an interesting read. One fascinating insight is given when Yorke was cross-examining a doctor called William George Frith who attended the Castle Hill meeting out of "curiosity." He had heard a lot about it and that morning had been in the company of a lady who urged him to go along. Yorke, she said, was going to make a very eloquent speech" and that he "is certainly sent by heaven to be the saviour of this country." The doctor finished with the barb:

"I know she and you have seen one another."

"What do you mean by that?" Yorke replied.

"I mean more intimate than is proper with a married woman."

"Is she pretty?"

"Yes. Very."

Yorke was found guilty and given a fine of two hundred pounds and two years' imprisonment at Dorchester prison. True to form, in gaol, he continued his way with the women, and developed a relationship with the daughter of the governor, marrying her on his release.

He returned to the law and carried on writing. He renounced his radical principles and was, thereafter, violently opposed to reform: Winifred says "he turned the Cat in the Pan."

His experience had left him embittered. He wrote an account of his trial and in it said he had "suffered more than any other man, under every species of obloquy, falsehood and calumny; not satisfied with inveighing against my public character, my private one was also to be assailed" and that he had not "gained one single friend from among the multitude who professed themselves friendly to reform, and having experienced more ill-usage from them than those of the opposite description."

According to Holland and Everett, Montgomery told of his surprise at Yorke appearing in Sheffield a few years later as a Lieutenant-Colonel in charge of a recruiting party, but instead of enlisting he was hooted out of the town.

❧❧❧

Winifred Left Behind

Winifred describes fainting on her return home from going to see Joseph one last time before he left. (She had ridden on horseback 18 miles there and 18 miles back and was 4 months pregnant at the time.) She was accompanied on this journey by Montgomery. Holland and Everett give a slightly different account. They have Winifred riding pillion behind the heroic Montgomery: "four hours in riding eight miles" to Newhill Grange, Wath-on-Dearne, the home of their friend, Joseph Payne. (Hartshead to Newhill Grange is actually about 12 miles.)

On Joseph's departure Winifred had an immediate problem –

how to run the business in his absence – as a woman, all access to cash ceased: she was unable to secure credit, and she could not enforce payment against people in credit to her. She had wages to pay and to pay duties on the Register in advance. One of the Gales' friends, William Shore, urged her to keep the business going and await Joseph's return, offering her a blank cheque to be repaid at a later date. He said: "Your friends all believe you competent to do so, and be assured it will everyday increase." After she had composed herself from her weeping, she declined. She saw it as her responsibility to join her husband abroad and decided to pay off creditors by selling the business. However, she accepted a £500 loan to be repaid from the property sale. James Montgomery went to London with the money to start settling affairs with creditors.

The following day while she was taking tea with James Eckroyd, a Quaker friend, and Benjamin Naylor, the minister at the Upper Chapel, one of the magistrates, Colonel Athorpe, called round with a constable. She assumed he had called round for some printing work which was being carried out and turned to ring the bell to the office when he informed her that the magistrates wanted to see her at the Tontine Inn. She writes: "Well," I answered somewhat impatiently, I confess, "they know where I live." "Yes madam," he replied, "but they sit as magistrates and bade me say 'they invite' rather than command your attendance." I told him, when I have taken my tea, then ready, I would go, for it was early in July, and the day long."

Not being sure whether she would be detained, she gave her friends instructions for looking after her family and the business. There were five magistrates and a clerk awaiting her at their room in the inn. She was questioned about Henry Yorke and the pamphlet that had been published containing his Castle Hill speech and whether it had been printed by them, or written whilst he was at their house. She answered cleverly – what we would call today a politician's answer – to avoid incriminating Yorke or her husband, but without telling a lie. After keeping her locked up for some time she was released. Outside the inn hundreds of men had gathered "with their smutty faces and leathern aprons on, as if they have been called from their forges, by some extreme cause." These men, supporters of the Galeses had vowed to pull down the Tontine if she had been detained. She got home to find that all their employees had also been taken away and questioned to find gaps in Winifred's account – however, not one of them told a story that was different to her, such was their loyalty.

She also tells of events which are reminiscent of the mob gathering around the Gales' house in September 1793, and indeed it seems she may be confusing them somewhat. However, it seems that in this period after Joseph's departure there was a similar attempt to intimidate the publishers of the *Register*. There was a similar response, and a rallying around her of supporters of reform who swore to protect her and posted an armed guard outside. She writes: "From this time until I left Sheffield, our nocturnal defenders, failed not to keep guard over us."

Winifred sold the newspaper to James Montgomery, who had obtained financial backing from Benjamin Naylor. They named the new newspaper *The Iris*. The running of the stationers and bookshop was to remain with the Gales sisters.

All the business affairs being settled, and preparations made for selling the house and possessions, she prepared to take her young family to join Joseph in Hamburg. The men in the printing office provided a bowl of punch so that everyone could drink farewell wishes to Winifred and Joseph. She left for Germany on the 25th of August on board the Britannia, seven months pregnant, with four children, and an orphan boy, John Clayton, who had worked for them in Sheffield and who wanted to go too.

Britain's Loss, America's Gain

Winifred's crossing to Hamburg was supposed to take four days. It was calm until they neared the coast at the Elbe and given the weather they risked not bringing a pilot on board at Cru Haven. This proved to be a big mistake as a thick fog came down and then a storm blew in and they had to continually tack to avoid the coast. Crates of crockery on board crashed and at midnight: "…the beds filled with water! When my poor child felt the element pouring upon him, he exclaimed, 'What did you bring me here for? Why didn't you leave me in Eckington, Mother?' Ah! why, indeed, I thought, but it may be God's will that we all go together!" The ship had sprung a leak. She prepared for death: "For my poor husband only did I feel – for his distress – his future desolation! I can truly aver, that personally I was not unhappy at this unexpected and melancholy termination of the hopes and fears of life; my dear children would not have to suffer and endure the loss of a mother's tender care."

The throwing overboard of heavy bales of woollen cloth stopped the ship sinking and the ship moved more steadily thereafter up the Elbe to Hamburg where they were met by a small boat leaving the shore with Joseph on board: "We met – language would poorly depict our mutual feelings!"

They went to live in Altona, now just a suburb of Hamburg with a family with whom Joseph had been lodging. They booked a passage to Philadelphia for the 17th September. On board the ship, Winifred was unhappy, she was feeling unwell and found the captain uncouth. Added to this, they got stuck in the Elbe unable to leave because of unfavourable winds. A thunderstorm followed: "a dreadful sight, quick and vivid lightnings, followed in such constant succession, that the whole hemisphere appeared in flames…" The final straw was a sailor being lost from the top mast where he had been ordered by the captain. In the end the Galeses decided to forfeit half of their passage money and send on their stowed books and clothes to be stored for later. They disembarked at Gluckstadt in a small pilot boat, into which Winifred was "carefully lowered in an armed chair" and returned to Hamburg. They decided to defer their departure and settled in Altona, after which they named their fifth child, a daughter, who was born that November. They endured a bitter winter in which the Elbe froze, mixing with intellectuals from around the continent and making preparations for their voyage in the Spring.

They left for Philadelphia on the 1st June 1795 on board the *William and Henry*; though the orphan boy, John Clayton, decided not to take the long voyage being consumptive and in poor health –

they paid his passage back to Hull.

(There is also a diary that was kept by Joseph Gales at this time, though it adds little detail to Winfred's – though anyone interested in what the weather was like on the crossing may find it illuminating. He refers to the ship as the *Charles and Henry* – which is probably correct as it seems a more contemporaneous account.)

The voyage across the Atlantic was not without incident. After weeks of the same routine, bowl after bowl of pea soup, weariness of the confined space, and sea-sickness on the part of Joseph, a sail was seen which turned out to be that of a "privateer" – pirates. They boarded the *William and Henry*, and captured the crew and captain. Winifred left Joseph, ill below decks, and went onto the deck with her baby. She ended up talking to two of the pirate crew, one of whom turned out to be originally from Yorkshire, and had not heard his native dialect for thirteen years. They conversed until sunset, Winifred expressing her fears that they would be taken to Bermuda, from where the pirate schooner sailed. She was reassured by the elder of the two, Lieutenant Bethel that she should not worry: "he owned one of the prettiest houses on the island, and that myself and my family should have a welcome asylum, with his own wife and children until we could get a passage to Philadelphia." The poor man had no chance – he received a lecture on how his wife must feel at his being a "voluntary follower of an execrable profession" ... "...in addition to the common dangers of a seafaring life, her husband, the father of her children had adopted a profession, in which the hand of every honest man was raised against him." She reduced him to tears. She apologized, but she: "did not regret having struck so forcibly on the nerve where better feelings are born."

The pirate captain, Hutchins, came to see her later to see the children "who are like angels in green and gold." As they slept, he: "passed his hand gently over their faces and stooped to kiss the little girls." He too was soon to feel the power of Winifred's censure, when he requested the letter bags and started to open the letters. "Your honourable profession, which rises every moment in my estimation – what! open private letters – explore family secrets – interfere with confidential communications – I am sorry to have witnessed it." The right they had to capture the *William and Henry* was then apparently "seriously discussed."

The upshot was that they were released and Winifred secured from the pirates a donation of some sugar molasses and flour. Afterwards, much relieved, the captain of the *William and Henry* described Hutchins as a bad man capable of every violation of decency and honour.

They met with violent storms of thunder and lightning, as they entered the Cape of Delamere, but finally set foot in Philadelphia on the 1ˢᵗ August 1795.

Just how great a loss Joseph Gales was (and who can doubt the importance of Winifred in that equation – they were very much a team) can be estimated from the valedictory message sent to Gales by the Constitutional Society, printed in Montgomery's *Iris*.

> "The eminent worth of your character, your important services to the great cause of human happiness, our irreparable injury in the life of so valuable a member, and persecution of which you are distinguished object – are so many loud calls for some testimonial our deep-felt sense of your merit, and our pungent grief at your sufferings.
>
> Yet, we are happy that we are not merely to speak the language of sympathetic condolence, but that of joy, of congratulation, and laudable envy.
>
> We rejoice to reflect, that the divine cause of truth and liberty has been supported by so unexceptionable, so able, and so successful an advocate.
>
> We cordially felicitate you on your escape from the insidious schemes and the enraged ferocity of cruel and inexorable men [...]
>
> We find consolatory pleasure in entertaining the idea that you will read these warm effusions of our souls, secure from oppression, and breathing the pure air of a free country, where the native and inalienable rights of man are known, respected, and enjoyed."

New World, New Beginnings

Joseph and Winifred Gales never returned to England. In Philadelphia Joseph took a job as a newspaper reporter and was the first reporter to publish verbatim accounts of the debates in Congress. He worked his way up and associated with Thomas Jefferson and Republican party leaders. He bought up an existing newspaper, the *Independent Gazetteer*, which he ran for a year. From Philadelphia, the Galeses went to Raleigh in North Carolina to set up a Republican supporting newspaper, *The Raleigh Register* which they ran for over thirty years, assisted in the early days by one Richard Davison, of "pikes-letter" fame.

Gales became a leading citizen in Raleigh, going on to become the Mayor of Raleigh from 1819-1833. His son, Joseph junior, also became a renowned newspaper man and was a partner in the *National Intelligencer* in Washington, and was Mayor of Washington from 1827-1830.

William Camage, William Broomhead and others were released without trial in December 1794 following a London jury's not guilty verdict on Thomas Hardy, though on condition they gave evidence in the later trial of Henry Yorke. There were jubilant celebrations on the streets of Sheffield to welcome their return.

James Montgomery, continued to publish the Iris for many years. In his first editorial he scorns the "imputation which would represent every reformer as a Jacobin, and every advocate for peace as an enemy to his King and Country." However, he expresses an intention to avoid "the influence of all party spirit" because any such declaration of political attachment might expose them "in the present times of alarm to obnoxious epithets and unjust and ungenerous reproaches."

Montgomery, however, faced worse than obnoxious epithets – within two years he had been prosecuted, convicted and imprisoned twice for printing seditious material and for libel. These trials were clearly a set-up, out of pique for not having succeeding in prosecuting Joseph Gales. The first time it was for publishing a supposedly libellous poem, first published in 1792, entitled "A

Patriotic Song," by a Clergyman of Belfast, celebrating the fall of the Bastille. Then in 1795 two people were killed and several injured when the local militia under the command of the Sheffield magistrates Colonel Athorpe attacked a crowd of demonstrators and opened fire. It was the report of this in the *Iris* (mild compared to the vitriol poured on Athorpe by Mather in his song *Norfolk Street Riots*) that led to Montgomery being tried for libel against Athorpe.

Later in life Montgomery obtained some prosecution papers which proved that these prosecutions were government inspired with a view "to put a stop to the associated clubs in Sheffield; and it is to be hoped, if we are fortunate enough to succeed in convicting the prisoner, it will go a long way towards curbing the insolence they have uniformly manifested." No doubt the acquittals of Hardy, Thelwall and other members of the London Society, were something that needed a correction. The second period of imprisonment damaged Montgomery's health and broke his morale.

The Iris continued but no longer as a radical newspaper in the same vein. Even while in prison Montgomery was writing to his acting editor urging him to stop all attacks on the Government and exercise extreme caution in covering local issues.

For a while the Constitutional Society remained active and open air meetings continued to be held into 1795, but not beyond this date.

In 1796 John Thelwall visited Sheffield and made contact with the Sheffield Society. He rejoiced in the intelligence and political awareness of the Sheffield members but observed that unlike the Norwich Society it had no leaders and was "a body without a head." He added that though several people of property and influence think with them, none had the courage to take their part and that as a consequence they were exposed to the petty tyranny of provincial persecution. In 1799 meetings of such societies were prohibited by the first of William Pitt's Combination Acts – the laws to ban the nascent trades unions.

However, that is not the end of the story. As Gales himself observed in January 1794 "Persecution cannot persuade the understanding even though it subdues the resolution." The people retained their political awareness. They met in private, talked, went under cover and waited. E.P. Thompson maintains that a consequence of Pitt's Combination Acts was to bring together the 'Jacobin' tradition represented by the Constitutional Societies and illegal trades unions. He continues that this was especially the case in Lancashire and Yorkshire, a movement which originated in Sheffield. He quotes a government informer who said that in Sheffield the Combination Act had stimulated a "general spirit of disaffection created in every class of artisan and mechanics by the late Bill [...]which I am afraid has already caused more to combine than would have thought of such a measure but for the Bills."

The repression continued for over 20 years and, as it eased, there was an upsurge of political activity and agitation for reform. Sheffield was at the forefront of such activities in the 1820s and 1830s including the Chartist Movement. One of the activists in these movements and an articulate spokesman for them was the poet Ebenezer Elliott the self styled "poet of the poor" who, commenting on his experience of being brought up in a radical dissenter household on the 1790s and early 1800s, wrote: "I have not forgot the English reign of terror, there you have the source of my political tendencies."

Sheffield continued to be at the forefront of radical political activity for the next 200 years up to and including the rate-capping campaign during the Thatcher government. It does not seem unreasonable to suggest that the stance of *The Sheffield Register* and the political consciousness engendered during its short life played a significant role in the formation of these attitudes and this tradition.

We will give Elliott the last word though he wrote in a later era. Referring to Sheffield he wrote:

"Town of the unbowed poor thou shalt not pine
Like the fall'n rustic, licensed rapine's thrall.
But, first to rise, wilt be the last to fall!"

References:

- *The Sheffield Register* 1787 to 1794,
- *The Sheffield Courant*, 1793-97,
- "Recollections" the Gales' memoir from the Gales Papers, 1799-1839, University of North Carolina Archives,
- Memoirs of the life and writings of James Montgomery, Holland, John, and James Everett, 1854-56
- The Editorial Experience of Joseph Gales, 1786-1794, Armytage, W. H. G. The North Carolina Historical Review 28, no. 3 (1951)
- The Freedom of Election: The Company of Cutlers in Hallamshire and the Growth of Radicalism in Sheffield, 1784-1792. Julie Macdonald, PhD thesis, University of Sheffield, 2005.
- From Sheffield to Raleigh: a Radical Publishing Network in the Age of Revolution, Michael James Daly, PhD thesis, Sheffield Hallam University Research Archive (SHURA): shura.shu.ac.uk/4075/
- The Making of the English Working Class, E.P Thompson, Pelican, 1982
- Artisans and Democrats: Sheffield in the French Revolution, John Stevenson, 1989
- Passages in the Life of Arthur Jewitt, 1844-1846, Manuscript, Edward Hall collection, EHC 172/M964, Wigan Archives
- Seditious Things: The Songs of Joseph Mather – Sheffield's Georgian Punk Poet, Steven Kay and Jack Windle
- Howells State Trials vol XXV
- Radical Citizens of the World, 1790-95, The Early Career of Henry Redhead Yorke, Journal of British Studies, Amanda Goodrich, 2014
- Letter from Colonel Oliver De Lancey, Home Office papers at the National Archives: HO 42/20 p. 394
- Sheffield in the Eighteenth Century, Robert Leader, 1901
- http://printprotestpoetry.group.shef.ac.uk/ for commentary on "The Observations of a Swine" and "Patriotism."

Acknowledgements

Professor William (Bill) Hampton (1930-2009), Dean of the Faculty of Educational Studies, Sheffield University for his valuable comments on my dad's draft.
Sheffield Libraries Local Studies Department – brilliant as always.
Adam James Smith, Honorary Research Fellow for the University of Sheffield's Centre for Archival Practices, and Lecturer in English at York St John University (and all-round good egg) for reading this through (twice!). Thanks for the kind comments and helpful suggestions.
Ruth, for rescuing all my dad's papers.

Dear reader

If you enjoyed reading *How Great a Crime*, it would be great if you could write a review on Amazon, Goodreads or whichever online sites you use: just a line or two would be great. I have no marketing department to provide support: reviews are all I have to promote this endeavour. Thanks!

My website www.1889books.co.uk contains information on my books.

The Evergreen in red and white is a novel about the first Romani gypsy to play for England: Rab Howell. Set in Sheffield in 1897-98, it follows Rab through his last turbulent year in the city as he struggles to do the right thing having fallen in love with another woman.

All Measures Necessary is my "political thriller" written in 2016 based on the ridiculous notion of what might happen if a left-wing, Labour leader became popular.

I have also published three other forgotten classics: *The Skipper's Wooing* by W W Jacobs, *Spirit of Old Essex,* a collection of works by Arthur Morrison, and *Put Yourself in his Place* by Charles Reade. *The Bantams of Sheffield* is Sheffield's second oldest novel and the first novel to feature the local dialect. *Historical Football Stories* is a collection of the oldest football (soccer) stories in the world, and *Joe Stepped off the Train* is a collection of short stories by a diverse group of authors from which all author royalties go to the charity *War Child.*

Seditious Things: The Songs of Joseph Mather- Sheffield's Punk Poet is a collection of Mather's songs and further background to this brilliant Sheffielder and contemporary of the Galeses.

Thanks.

You can get in touch via facebook.com/SteveK1889, Twitter.com/SteveK1889 or e-mail me at stevek1889@gmail.com

Printed in December 2022
by Rotomail Italia S.p.A., Vignate (MI) - Italy